Grassroots Governance

Grassroots Governance

Gram Sabha in West Bengal

Amal Mandal

RAWAT PUBLICATIONS

Jaipur • New Delhi • Bangalore • Hyderabad • Guwahati

ISBN 978-81-316-0492-2

The publication of this book was financially supported by the ICSSR. The responsibility for the facts stated, opinions expressed, or conclusions reached, is entirely that of the author and that the ICSSR accepts no responsibility for them.

ICSSR Consultant: Professor Ramashray Roy, BM 36, Shalimar Bagh (East), Delhi

Published by
Prem Rawat for **Rawat Publications**
Satyam Apts., Sector 3, Jawahar Nagar, Jaipur 302 004 (India)
Phone: 0141 265 1748 / 7006 Fax: 0141 265 1748
E-mail: info@rawatbooks.com
Website: www.rawatbooks.com

New Delhi Office
4858/24, Ansari Road, Daryaganj, New Delhi 110 002
Phone: 011-23263290

Also at *Bangalore, Hyderabad* and *Guwahati*

Typeset by Rawat Computers, Jaipur
Printed at Nice Printing Press, New Delhi

To Manjima and Sayan
for encouragement and inspiration

Contents

Preface

One assertion, however contesting, is that governance is continually and sharply declining in India. Not only the convicted leaders are assuming reign of the states, the phenomena of criminalisation, corruption and dominance of '*crore-patis*' have also reached enormous proportion. When political leaders behave in irresponsible, insensitive and corrupt ways, the erosion of governance gets vindicated. In view of the fact that the political system is not only conditioned by the conduct of the political leaders but it also shapes their behaviour, there is need to reform it so as to improve the process of governance and restore democracy in both word and spirit. One option is to put in place constant checks and balances and strong public accountability.

At the lowest stratum of Indian political system, an innovative and potentially revolutionary experiment is going on in the frame of the Gram Sabha, which is often touted as the unrivalled and virtuous grassroots institution that can not only redirect the panchayat system, but also resurrect the otherwise deficient Indian democratic governance. Though it is a long standing institution, it has evoked positive expectations, particularly since the constitutionalisation of panchayats in 1993: after all, 1999–2000 and 2009–10 have already been celebrated as the 'Year of Gram Sabha'. The Gram Sabha seems to have epitomised the devolution drive to deepen democracy at the grassroots as it charts out the 'public sphere' where open deliberation and collective decision-making will expectedly ensure participatory and accountable local governance.

Since the Gram Sabha is an exclusive and virtuous institution, an empirical assessment of its working and impacts on rural development and rural governance in a state like West Bengal assumes importance for many reasons. West Bengal is arguably the only state that has undertaken (and sustained) comprehensive decentralisation for which the structure and process of rural power has reportedly been reshaped where the villagers in general, and marginal groups in particular, have been empowered, enthused and are intimately involved in the decision-making process of panchayat institutions. As the ambience here is supposed to be more conducive than elsewhere, the potentialities of the Gram Sabha are likely to come to fruition more indicatively in the state of West Bengal.

I am grateful to the Indian Council of Social Science Research, New Delhi for supporting and sponsoring the research project without which this book could not have been possible. Two research assistants, namely, Niranjan Mandal and Manab Bhatta, undertook the gruelling task of collecting the primary data and information through village survey and they also provided few insights. The comments of Professor Ramashray Roy, Dr Arun K. Jana and Dr Jayata Goswami on the draft helped considerably in fine-tuning the presentation. For all the support and cooperation received from the members of the Gram Sabha, elected Gram Panchayat members and Gram Panchayat officials, I place on record my deep sense of indebtedness and appreciation.

Abbreviations and Glossary

BDO	Block Development Officer, administrative head of a block (unit below sub-division)
BJP	Bharatiya Janata Party
BPL	Below the Poverty Line
CDP	Community Development Programmes
CPM	Communist Party of India (Marxist)
DL&LRO	District Land and Land Reforms Officer
GoI	Government of India
GoWB	Government of West Bengal
GP	Gram Panchayat, the lowest panchayat tier at village level
GS	Gram Sabha, unitary village assembly at GP level
GUS	Gram Unnayan Samity, one "administrative arm" of Gram Sansad, established in West Bengal by the Panchayat Amendment Act, 2003
IAY	Indira Awas Yojana
ICDS	Integrated Child Development Services

JRY	Jawahar Rojgar Yojna
LFG	Left Front Government (in West Bengal)
MLA	Member of Legislative Assembly (of state)
MP	Member of Parliament
NES	National Extension Services
NGO	Non-Governmental Organisation
NREGS	National Rural Employment Guarantee Scheme (of states) (now prefixed by Mahatma Gandhi)
NSSO	National Sample Survey Organization
OAP/IGNOAPS	Old Age Pension (now Indira Gandhi National Old Age Pension Scheme)
OBC	Other Backward Classes
PESA	Panchayat (Extension to the Scheduled Areas) Act, 1996
Pradhan/ Sarpanch	GP President is known as Pradhan in West Bengal and in North Indian states as Sarpanch
PRIs	Panchayati Raj Institutions
PS	Panchayat Samity, the middle tier of panchayat at each administrative block
Sabha	Gram Sabha (in West Bengal)
Sansad (Gram)	The statutory plebeian forum of the electorate at every constituency of GP of West Bengal
SC	Scheduled Caste
SGRY	Sampoorna Grameen Rozgar Yojana
SHG	Self-help Group
ST	Scheduled Tribe
TMC	Trinamul Congress
UNDP	United Nations Development Programme
WB	West Benbal
ZP	Zilla Parishad

1

In Search of Breakthrough

India is a land of contrast and paradox, continually maintaining a hiatus between rhetoric and reality, theory and practice or avouchment and affliction. Periodic proclamations regarding amelioration of woes and injustice may apparently be emboldening but they more often hoodwink the people. The pledges are for public consumption and are fulfilled more in breaches. The euphoria over new public policy, programmes replacing earlier ones soon ends up in a whimper. There are only a few oases of positive action and hope amidst the vast desert of despondency and inertia. The more one delves deep into one political stratum, the more enigmas one encounters.

India is one of a few developing countries that has embarked on and successfully maintained a democratic form of governance. Despite considerable odds, democracy in India is thriving and showing remarkable resilience. Its success is stark staring when considered against many benchmarks and the experience of even matured Western democracies.[1] The relatively stable and successful Indian experiment flies in the face of many theories of comparative politics which predict a doom of democracy in a country having low economic development, high inequality and social diversity (Ganguly et al., 2007: xi). India strongly refutes several conjectures about the prerequisites of a democracy where a poverty-stricken, cleavage and faction-ridden society is supposed to be one unfit case for sustaining a democratic system or where the sharp social heterogeneity and tumultuous divisions are likely to induce either a weak government or an authoritarian regime. With 15 general elections and 7 changes in the Union Government through the ballot box verdict, even the sterner critics have to acknowledge India's outstanding achievement in the maintenance of democracy and civil liberty.

Having trans-cultural dimensions and transcendental character touching almost every fundamentals of social life, democracy has two basic paradigms—as a process or condition and as a method and modality. Fairly distinguishable is democracy as an ideal of political association (thus a value in itself) and as a system of governance (or as a means to achieve the end). As an ideal, democracy denotes power of the people in wider sense where everyone controls decision-making and execution process. Everybody holds power, each is to obey oneself and nobody is subject to anybody else. It is the political philosophy for good governance and recognition of liberty, equality and dignity of individuals. As a system, democracy implies a series of rules, regulations which support a system of power. Certain procedures and standardisation are accepted in a specific power system.

However, democracy is not all about formation of the government or representation but also about how the government works and what it achieves, how it translates the commitment to and assuages the woes of the people and how far it ensures emancipation and promotes a dignified life for the people. Notwithstanding few positives concerning the procedural aspects, India has a rather dismal record of following much of the ideals of democracy. Democracy may have taken roots amidst a low-income economy, widespread poverty, illiteracy, ethnic diversity and absence of civic culture, but the success is more about institutionalisation and certainly less on noteworthy accomplishment or outcome. Massive impoverishment, power hungry politicians, overburdened and inefficient judiciary, disrespect to laws, widespread corruption, biased media, growing fundamentalism all make a mockery of the otherwise touted Indian democracy.

People have got voting right, they queue up in voting booths and elect their representatives. But the gullible people remain hungry, illiterate and they hardly have the power to influence the policy of the government. It is, as Jayaprakash Narayan once castigated, more like an inverted pyramid standing on its head and the democracy connoting mere a government by consent. The hapless masses carry the burden of democracy while the elected representatives corner and enjoy the fruits (of power). Once elected, the representatives tend to harbour haughty, megalomaniac, narcissist and authoritarian attitude towards the common people, become all-knowing masters, enjoy larger-than-life and demigod status and act as the benefactor. After elections they often pursue parochial and even predatory policies—sometimes push those with brutal state power in the face of public opposition (land acquisition).

The accountability—the cherished principle of democracy—has by and large proved porous or hollow. The electorate do not generally see their representatives except during election times. After elections, representatives arrogate to themselves the right to what constitutes the priority or preference of the people, show scant respect to the laws and accountability. The growing phenomenon of super-rich and representatives with criminal antecedent[2] raise the question on how they can represent the people and bring about socio-economic progress. They may be insensitive to basic human rights (education) or cannot agree on progressive legislation (reservation for women), but they unite in securing benefits for themselves[3] or blocking any threat to their position.

Indian democracy is lurching from one challenge to another, from one crisis to another. The machinery of government is increasingly getting isolated from popular control, producing a crisis of accountability. The institutional capacity to deal with conflict and solve problems is declining (Kohli, 1987: 17). Explicit is the move towards centralisation and homogenisation of power (Kothari, 1988: 188) that impinges on individual freedom and creativity. Fragmentation and proliferation of parties, mostly in terms of leaders' personal equation to power, has its adverse impact on a stable government and sound policy. Those who get and wield power are determined to hold on to power and are averse to downward percolation.

The development of institutions and practices that make democracy real has its impacts on distortion, deviation and downgrading of people's power. The political party—a realistic means to represent people's will and to run a government—has evolved as the power centre, supplanting public control. Parties, as in most representative democracies, are more like a professional political organisation with their own rules, selection procedure, hierarchy, client-base and they are emerging as the enterprise designed and devoted to conquering and maintaining power.[4] The party getting majority support in elections forms the government and tends to embody and represent the people.[5] The party in the government claims to know what is best for the state and people and takes policy decisions. In this context, two specific quagmires are: how far the party in the government represents the people and how plausible is the principle where the winning party takes all and the losing party loses all.[6]

What the otherwise celebrated Indian democracy has offered to the common men can be comprehended by the incidence of poverty. The poverty estimates[7] for 2004–05, made by NSSO, 61st Round on uniform 60 days recall period, disclosed that 28.3 per cent in rural, 25.7 per cent in urban and 27.5 per cent of total Indian population were living below the poverty line, that is drawing on per capita per month consumption of ₹ 356.30 for rural and 538.60 for urban areas at all-India level which is the weighted average of the state specific poverty lines. In other words, total 306 million people (220 million in rural) were officially regarded as poor. Another way of looking at poverty scenario is to consider the food insecurity. Regarding perceived food insecurity among rural households, NSSO, 61st round revealed that 2.5 per cent in

Kerala and Chhattisgarh, 3.2 per cent in Bihar, 5.9 per cent in Orissa, 11.7 per cent in West Bengal and 2.5 per cent households in India faced food insecurity.[8]

Uninterrupted political democracy with regular elections and ingrained faith on democratic process when contrasted with widespread illiteracy, ill-health, malnutrition, out-migration, institutionalised corruption, absence of basic needs like food, shelter for the masses, one cannot but marvel at the 'remarkable achievement'. An entrenched political democracy with socio-economic disparities and deprivation makes Indian case a clear deviation from the stereotypes of parliamentary democracy. India probably contains the contours and characteristics that may be typified as a new model unparalleled in the Western discourse.

The anomalies and challenges bedevilling Indian democracy are not, however, exclusive. Similar trends are manifesting in other liberal democracies around the world. Though democracy is supposed to be the best form of political organisation that human society has so far evolved, many gaps and deficiencies are increasingly unfolding almost everywhere. If the spread and quantity of democracy is indubitably emphatic, the same cannot be claimed for its meaning, quality and outcome.

In the words of Fung and Wright (2001: 5): the institutional form of liberal democracy seems increasingly ill-suited to the present-day problems. Democracy as a way of organising the state has come to be narrowly identified with territorially based competitive elections of political leadership for legislative and executive offices. The mechanism of political representation seems ineffective in accomplishing the central ideal of democratic politics: facilitating active political involvement of citizenry, forging political consensus through dialogue, devising and implementing public policy that foster a productive economy and healthy society, and distribute benefits to all citizens.

Commonly perceptible is the antipathy of people in getting involved in the political process. Many empirical studies substantiate the marked decline in citizen's political participation. The number of people taking membership of political organisations and electorate turning out in voting booths is ebbing, not only in national but also in local governments where they have direct concern.[9] The public opinion researches refer to an increasing loss of public confidence, a growing distance between citizens and the government, and this is considered as a symptom of a crisis.[10] One assertion is that the gaps had never been greater between the decision made by those in power and the wishes of the people, between democratic practices and public aspiration and emancipation. It is the nadir of representative democracy, which has been hijacked by 'elite democracy'. Demonstrative is the diminished democracy in which public involvement has lost its link to political life. A downsizing of democracy is getting evident where collective citizen action has given away to narrow interest groups. Few noticeable deficits of democracy, as summarised by Luckham et al. (2000: 22–23) include: (i) hollow citizenship where people do not enjoy equal rights and entitlement, (ii) lack of vertical accountability where citizens are unable to hold government and political elites accountable for their use of power and (iii) weak horizontal accountability where executives manipulate checks and balances through patronage, corruption and repress dissent.

Connecting the Missing Link

In the face of chasm and crisis, a number of competing strands are emerging in which deepening democracy is one approach.[11] Arising out of the tradition of participatory democracy, deepening democracy goes beyond the set of rules, procedures, institutional design and harps on the process through which citizen can gain substantial control over the decision-making. It intends to extend democracy itself through creation and supporting more participatory mechanism of citizen engagement which in turn is built on and supports a robust view of rights and responsibilities of democratic citizenry. Accepting that conventional representative democracy does not provide sufficient opportunity to citizen in influencing the affairs of the state, the emphasis here is on political project of developing and sustaining more substantial and empowered citizen participation in the political process (Gaventa, 2006: 7). The objective is to change the balance of power between citizen and state through the promotion of direct and meaningful participation in governance.

A number of initiatives around the world are being attempted to find new forms of governance linking citizen and state in a new way and rebuilding the relationship between citizen and government. Such efforts are mostly at the local level which is historically regarded as the key site for democracy building and citizen participation, and where people come to intimate and continuous contact with politicians and activities of the state. In India one such reform initiative culminates at the village level where the statutorily ordained Gram Sabha (village assembly) is expected to script a new era of governance.

In view of non-responsiveness and under-performance of the state, a solution is sought through decentralisation, or its recent incarnation—democratic decentralisation, which is expected to entrench democracy, public-centric development and responsive mode of governance.

Decentralisation first appeared in administrative literature as a response to the vices of centralised administration, and economic planning is ambiguous in its meaning. Four different categories—deregulation, deconcentration, devolution and privatisation—are often used to describe the process of decentralisation and to differentiate the type of sectoral arrangements. A further analytical tool has been prescribed: administrative, fiscal, political dimension of decentralisation. Administrative decentralisation means partial/full transfer of administrative responsibilities. Fiscal decentralisation is about shift in financial power (sometime authority) to generate local revenue. And political decentralisation refers to transfer of political authority through the establishment of representative local government. Political analysts emphasise on political components and public choice literature focuses on fiscal issues. The result is that a framework incorporating all possible dimensions of decentralisation and their inter-linkage is seldom evident. However, given the overall experience, it is quite easy to undermine or render one type of decentralisation redundant by fore-closing other element(s): political decentralisation without administrative and/or fiscal decentralisation can be superfluous.

More expressive and less ambiguous is the democratic decentralisation.[12] When 'democratic' is added to decentralisation as one adjective or as prefix, a significant change in the context, content and thrust is impacted. Democratic decentralisation differs from majority of decentralisation initiatives taken since 1950s which were mainly administrative reforms without substantial democratic component. Three specific dimensions are considered 'heart' of democratic decentralisation: autonomy, participation and accountability. Through participation local citizens would get meaningful role in local decisions affecting them directly, thereby they would be able to insert inputs into what local governments do. Through accountability, people would hold local governments responsible for the exercise of power, see what governments have done or left undone. By building participation and accountability, local governments are to be more responsive to local people's desires and problems, etc. Thus, the efficacy of service delivery will improve. In this way democratic decentralisation combines the devolutionary form of decentralisation (transfer of power) and democracy at local level. As Manor (1999: 7) maintained, decentralisation without democratisation can only be incomplete and non-conducive to socially effective result.[13] Democratic decentralisation is a meaningful devolution to lower stratum that is accessible and accountable to local people (Blair, 2000). Something more that downward delegation of authority, democratic decentralisation is a system of governance where people would possess the right to bring public functionaries and officials to account as through elections and other collective actions. Here the state apparatus gets exposed and is made responsible to local aspiration, thus producing a system of governance that is more effective.

Democratic decentralisation strives for a reciprocal relationship between central (union or provinces) and local governments and local citizenry. It offers the people to discuss, decide, devise and implement policies, extends democratisation and deepens the democratic process.[14] Democratic decentralisation seems to be an attempt at convergence of decentralisation and democratic local governments with the objective of regenerating the state in a democratic way. This political dimension is significant as it facilitates a process through which diverse local interests can be negotiated, aggregated and resource allocation can be made in a deliberative and responsive manner. Shaking off the age-old image of service delivery mechanism, local governments transcend to institutions that enable local people to take decisions by themselves and for themselves. By offering political freedom and opportunity to participate in decision-making, it triggers a 'virtuous cycle' of development where people would be able to chart out their own course of development. Conviction is that governance does matter for development, as the failure of many development programmes reflects a failure of governance (UNDP, 2002: 51).

The Indian Initiative

Regarding local governments, India offers one absorbing, if not somewhat wavering story. To cut a long story short, the British government introduced statutory rural local government that obliterated 'communitarian' panchayats. Though the declared intention, as in the famous Ripon Resolution 1882, was to associate people in civic services and to extend democratic principle, the real objective of the British government was something different.[15] The local self-government, as is understood in liberal discourse, actually emerged during the later part of British rule in India.

Despite the legacy of British mode of local governments, constitutional provision (Art. 40) and public policy emphasis (as in first Five-Year Plan), the state governments tinkered with the establishment of rural self-governments. It is only after the recommendations of Balawantrai Mehta Committee report (1957) and consequent active enthusiasm of Prime Minister Nehru and his community development minister S.K. Dey, the advent of the Panchayati Raj Institutions (hereafter *only* PRIs) as the unit of rural self-governments could kick-start.

B. Mehta Committee suggested three-tier PRIs at gram (village), block and district levels and it repeatedly called the envisaged structure as democratic decentralisation. The Committee's conceptualisation was indeed comprehensive: devolution of certain functions and responsibilities as listed in the report itself, direction to the states not to operate on those devolved matters, if at all only through the organs of local authority (p. 6). Yet, the Committee did not go for decentralised polity. It was obsessed with successful implementation of Community Development Programmes (CDP) and National Extension Services (NES) and this prompted the Committee to confer pivotal role to the middle tier panchayat that was coterminous with NES block. Moreover, the Committee recommended devolution of only developmental functions to panchayats and kept regulatory ones for bureaucracy. Ironically, such differentiation of functions for separate authorities continues to haunt panchayats, for which they are yet to evolve as full-fledged local self-governments.

It is noteworthy that the 'first generation panchayats' soon lost shine in most states. The initial euphoria and zeal evaporated and the strong indication is that panchayats had made a downhill slide soon after the demise of Prime Minister Nehru. A number of factors and developments conspired to their stagnation and decline. Meagre assigned functions, weak resource base, elite capture of power, corruption, inefficiency, political interference, parochial loyalty and power concentration all seriously limited the role and utility of PRIs (GoI, 1978: 67). The crux was the enmity shown by the higher level elites (MP, MLAs) who perceived in the emergence of panchayat leadership a threat to their position in their respective constituencies. L.M. Singhvi Committee (1986) had ferreted few other factors: denial of national priority, lack of continuous process of research, evolution and feedback and course correction. PRIs had to struggle for survival with the institutions of established power. The elected elites and bureaucracy visualised in the emerging panchayat leadership a competing cadre and they were reluctant to cooperate or socialise with them.

From 2 October, 1959 when the first panchayat was inaugurated till the passage of the 73rd Constitution Amendment Act, 1992 (hereafter 73rd Amendment), PRIs were virtually dead and gone (barring Maharashtra and Gujarat). However, during this period the initiatives taken particularly by two state governments were inspiriting. After assuming state power, the Left Front government (hereafter *only* LFG) in West Bengal conducted panchayat elections on 4 June, 1978 and this aroused new hope about the potential redistributive and developmental role that panchayat can perform. Later on, Janata Party government under R.K. Hegde introduced one 'robust' panchayat system in Karnataka. Moreover, Telegu Desam party held panchayat elections in Andhra Pradesh during 1987. Interestingly, in all three states the ruling parties happened to be regional ones without having ties with the ruling party or coalition at the centre and all states allowed open participation of political parties in the panchayat elections, indicating certain political calculi involved in the regenerative efforts.

At the same time, the justification for and urgency of constitutional backing to panchayat was steadily gaining ground. As per the original constitutional scheme, the states had the absolute authority relating to the constitution, holding election, devolution of powers and even abolition of PRIs. Because of such wider latitude, states dilly-dallied and even strangulated panchayat system, without being warned or brought to book. Constitutional ordination was supposed to be crucial for averting states' quiescence and for elevating panchayats to a commanding height.

After few abortive attempts, Indian parliament finally passed the 'historic' 73rd amendment act (with effect from 24 April, 1993). For the first time, PRIs got constitutional status, conceptual redirection, uniform structure, permanent entity and significant powers. This central act enjoins the states to constitute panchayat at village, intermediate (block) and district levels and to endow them with powers and authority necessary for enabling them to function as institutions of self-government and to devolve powers and responsibilities with respect to the preparation of plans and implementation of schemes for economic development and social justice (Art. 243G (a) (b)). Apparently, the amendment makes a significant shift from erstwhile local self-government to the institution of self-government, transforms the Indian government structure into three distinct strata and above all, fills the long persisting political vacuum below the state.

Together with constitutional recognition, the act entails inclusionary provisions whereby the traditionally excluded and vulnerable sections of Indian society get the statutory chance to participate and hold seats and posts in PRIs. Panchayat seats and executive posts therein are now statutorily reserved for: (i) SCs and STs in proportion to their population in the area concerned, (ii) women, to the extent of one-third of total seats and posts (including the share in SC and ST category) and (iii) Backward Classes, if the state deems it necessary. Thus, the act widens the participatory planks and ingrains democratisation.

Core Questions

Among all the provisions of the 73rd Amendment, arguably the most important one having wider ramifications and far-reaching impacts on the process of rural development and governance relates to the Gram Sabha. Despite curt reference to it in the central act, all the state governments have consequently established the Gram Sabha (hereafter *only* GS) as one integral component of the Gram Panchayat (hereafter *only* GP). Some states like West Bengal, Kerala and Madhya Pradesh have also experimented with GS by conferring extraordinary powers and involving it in decentralised planning, programme implementation, decision-making and village governance.

From the outset, GS has created enthusiasm and evoked affective feelings. For about a decade, commentaries and writings came out incessantly, surpassing other facets of PRIs. Those having a mooring in Gandhian teaching found their dream of people-centric governing unit come true. Policy makers and governments also joined in the celebration—1999–2000 and later on 2009–2010 have been observed as the 'Year of Gram Sabha', a distinction so far denied to the parental panchayat structures. Verily, GS is said to be one virtuous institution having the potential to revitalise the panchayat system, resurrect the otherwise deficient democratic governance and it is one unrivalled and somewhat audacious experiment at the grassroots.

This assembly of electorate at the village level is expected to bring about myriad transmutations: impacting a significant breakthrough in the conventional representative form of governance, implanting wider base of panchayats and redirecting rural development process. Political decision-making power directly to the villagers can establish people's *raj*, replacing the conventional representative *raj*. GS seems to be one epoch making institution that can transform the very character of Indian democracy, edify 'direct' democracy or 'participatory' democracy. Being the embodiment of 'direct democracy', as Singhvi Committee (1986) contended, GS will renew the republican base of Indian democracy. GS is an institution of 'direct' democracy, 'village democracy', which, by intensifying popular sovereignty, tends to embody Athenian variety of democracy. GS is the base, soul, fountainhead on which the entire edifice of Indian democracy can be built. Some regard GS as the epitome of and the very concept is based on the Gandhian formulation of *Gram Swaraj* (village self-rule). As an umbrella organisation, GS has important role in activating the democratic process at the grassroots, in inculcating community spirit, in increasing political awareness, in educating people in administrative and political processes and in enabling the weaker sections to progressively assert their viewpoints.

Following the postulates of parliamentary democracy, GS is also reckoned as the general assembly, the legislature having the power to frame policy decisions while Gram Panchayat (GP) will be its executive arm or the cabinet being responsible to the legislature, where the budget and accounts of GP are to be placed, development programmes deliberated and beneficiaries for public schemes selected. Rajni Kothari (1998: 190) has visualised GS as the watchdog that can obviate the politician-bureaucratic nexus by forcing it to be responsible and accountable. With the active involvement of people, GS will oversee the work of the elected body (GP), browbeat the dominance of a particular group or caste. Kothari has also contended that the position of rural poor will not improve so long the decision-making power remains out of their reach and the poor do not gain a stake in state power and use it against their traditional exploiters.

From development perspective, the active involvement of the villagers in the decision-making process is likely to ensure that their perceived priorities get in the development decisions, the efficacy of programme implementation improves and programme benefits reach to the deserving people. Being one participatory forum, GS will facilitate development from below by evolving need based, realistic local plans on the basis of village agro-economy, ecology and socio-economic conditions. Conceptually, GS is the forum where civic engagement and formation of social capital is possible and will hopefully be realised.

GS brings local governments closer to people. With the opened up opportunity there would be enlightened, responsible and proactive participation of the people in GP affairs, which will ensure transparency, accountability, responsiveness and popular control over the decision-making and implementation process. Having institutionalised people's participation, GS is set to legitimise the authority of PRIs, enhance transparency in panchayat functioning and inculcate respect for and receptivity to political institutions and leadership. GS is supposed to be the panacea capable of curing almost all kinds of failings and fallacies of decentralisation. The effective and successful role on the part of GS will restore the missing link and reinvigorate the panchayat system. There will expectedly be close relationship between well-performing GS and proper-functioning panchayat institutions, as the 2nd Administrative Reforms Commission (2007) contemplated.

The perceptible trend is to treat GS as one primary and basic unit of village governance. Almost all public schemes/programmes are now incorporating a direction to involve GS in deciding projects, selecting beneficiaries and overseeing the implementation process—the latest example being National Rural Employment Guarantee Scheme (of states). Moreover, one proposed act of Ministry of Rural Development, Government of India intends to offer comprehensive statutory backing to panchayats and GS. The (Draft) Model Panchayat and Gram Swaraj Act, 2009 proposes five-tier panchayat structure: district, block and village panchayat and Gram Sabha and Ward Sabha. As per this act, there will be uniform two-tier GS—one composite and another at every ward/constituency of GP. The Act details the functions, powers and duties of Ward Sabha and Gram Sabha[16] and these are more akin to those specified for the 5th Schedule (tribal) areas. Besides the general issue of governance, GS is also supposed to play pivotal role in such intractable problems of human civilisation as climate change.[17]

Surely, the concept of an assembly of electorate has, unlike any other unit of panchayat, received focal attention, attracted wide adulatory references, raised expectations on many fronts and has created bravura that sometimes borders on euphoria. Perhaps GS has evoked more hopes and aspirations than it possibly can or is presently capable of fulfilling.

Of course, GS was in operation in some states. Noteworthy is the fact that during the pre-73rd Amendment era all the central level committees that reviewed and suggested measures for strengthening democratic decentralisation pointed out disquieting features and dismal role of GS (Rau, 2001: 186). And none, even when headed by noted Gandhians, recommended for statutory recognition to GS. Diwankar Committee (GoI, 1963), set up exclusively to "suggest measure necessary to ensure that Gram Sabha is built up as the base of Panchayati Raj" favoured gradual strengthening in line with PRIs themselves. "In spite of its importance, it would take time for the organisation (GS) to grow and gather strength, even if statutory provisions were made to transfer power to it" the committee contended (p. 14). On this backdrop, when GS gets constitutional recognition (however woolly) and when it pervades the political landscape, one core question is whether the earlier reasoning and reluctance was misplaced or momentary or whether the situation has changed radically justifying the surge of GS.

The extent and nature of functional devolution and operational ambience of PRIs in general and GP in particular assume importance because the powers and functions of GS go hand in hand with those. In other words, are the powers of GP comprehensive enough and conducive for people-centric development? How far GS has been assigned with powers and responsibilities over which the people have direct stake and unencumbered control is critical for realising most of the developmental roles expected of GS.

Another aspect is how the establishment and eminence of GS is affecting the functioning of GP. Induction of two authorities—as legislature, executive or whatever—having jurisdiction over the same subjects must have administrative and political underpinnings. The conventional apprehension was that one powerful GS could compromise the administrative efficiency of GP. How is the popular control over GP members improving or impeding the decision-making process of GP?

Another related issue is what have been the reception and response of GP members and the political leadership to GS as one village institution. Do they perceive GS as an onslaught on their political clout? Do villagers, conversely, feel empowered, put forth demands and try to control the decision-making power of GP? In case public demands are placed at GS forum, how are these being received, incorporated in and acted upon by GP? Whether or not GP members try to manipulate the public voice or demand and whether or not they try to call the shots from behind.

However counterproductive it may be, the overall Indian political experience authenticates that the electorate feel contended after casting votes and they tend to remain nonchalant thereafter. And the elected representatives regard decision-making as their exclusive preserve. If and when the people try to audit the performance, set the development agenda at GS parlance, this is likely to interfere with the supposed prerogative of the politicians. The operationalisation of GS depends on the assumption that people are willing and will be evincing interest after electing their representatives and they will exercise political control even in the face of opposition from GP members.

It is generally acquiesced that the society that has not extensive social democracy or that has not internalised the norms of democracy can hardly aspire for a village assembly that can act orderly, collectively and creatively. When disorder and disruptions rule the roost in the highly protected and pampered legislatures, will not a free-for-all situation aggravate the prospect of GS?

GS is basically based on the notion of community or communitarianism. The assembly members are expected to be committed to and concerned with community concerns. But anthropological and sociological researches reveal almost ubiquitous divisions, hierarchy and cleavages based on caste, class, gender and land based patron-client relationship. Such studies harp on the fact that Indian rural society is torn horizontally and vertically, they warn against romantic view on villageism and cast doubt on all-village institution. The introduction of local, civic and criminal administration during the British rule disrupted the social fabric, which has subsequently been bulldozed by the state-induced development interventions and pervasive politicisation. The proliferating polycentric institutions and pluralistic clusters are further fragmenting the community character and homogeneity of interests. True, changes are taking place, but they have not yet eliminated the divisions, exclusion, inequity, etc. Any village assembly has to operate in the matrix pervaded by socio-economic and political divisions and heterogeneity which cannot be conjured out of existence by legislative fiat or wishful thinking.

The failure of panchayats to entrench good governance and the success of community based initiatives has reinforced the faith on self-governance by the village community. Such faith is premised on few crucial yet untested hypotheses. The development efforts can be successful and sustainable when the villagers, more so the marginal sections, are directly involved in the formulation and implementation of the decisions affecting themselves. The villagers will be able to organise and acquire voice and vibes. Notwithstanding the schism of caste, class, gender or politics, one village community exists and it will act collectively and responsively if given legal and institutional space. This collective village forum would be an effective vehicle of good governance, implying that an honest, transparent, pro-poor system will gain head when the elected representatives and bureaucrats are made responsible to the people. And the political leadership will sustain the assembly and it would be receptive to and take cognisance of the popular demands and directions.

Conceptual Frame and Methodology

The exclusive and somewhat audacious institutional innovation at the grassroots is supposed to have proverbial potential and poignant possibilities. GS is expected to revitalise and redirect the panchayat system. The general reckoning is that the failure of panchayat was due to lack of involvement of people in the scheme of local governance and if and when GS gets going strongly, most of the dysfunctionalities of PRIs would begin to evaporate. The decision-making power directly to the rural electorate and the accountability of the elected representatives would offer the villagers, more so the marginalised sections, their own brand of 'socialism'. Whether such expectations are realistic or utopian require to be assessed by ground testing of the nuances of the working of GS or by an objective stock of the operational experience and dynamics of GS. And such an inquiry can be indicative when the locale is West Bengal, a state having relatively entrenched and successful 'political panchayat' system.

The basic conceptual frame of the study is that the Gram Sabha and Gram Sansad—two distinct but integral components of GS in West Bengal—have comprehensive powers and functions and these village assemblies engage and enable the villagers to participate for directing and reinforcing local governance. When the panchayats, the institutional manifestation of democratic decentralisation in rural India, are sometimes regarded as local governance institutions, the rejuvenated GS has enlarged the participatory character of panchayats as well as the process of local democracy. GS, appertaining to one assembly of the rural electorate or one collective popular forum recognised, endowed and protected by the state panchayat act, affords the villagers the opportunity to participate, discuss, deliberate, decide and manage their collective affairs.

GS straightway holds out the scope for, indeed requires people's active participation, implying a close and continuous involvement of the people in the socio-economic and political issues affecting their lives and an engagement and act through which people would seek on equal terms to influence and gain control over the decision-making process. Such participation has to uphold the right to equality, information and contestability and the right to hold the elected members answerable for the use of authority and resources. In conformity with the consequential framework (Blair, 2000: 23), the people's participation is for governing their affairs. The local or grassroots governance refers to the process of establishing democratic local government institution that is responsible, responsive and accountable to the electorate and a process that facilitates the electorate to influence and direct the formulation and implementation of the policies and programmes over which the local institution has statutory jurisdiction.

Though almost every policy document now avouches for participation of people accepting it as one virtuous cycle, it is important to emphasis that several factors and conditions affect and determine the participation of people (Conyers, 2008: 30): whether participation is respected and based on equality, whether the issue for participation concerns the people directly and intimately, whether participants receive support in order to meet individual demands, whether participants have fair amount of knowledge, time, skill and competence.

Similarly, the establishment of local government is not an *ipso facto* guarantee for responsible, accountable or effective governance. The functional devolution which in most cases tends to be either partial or rhetorical is one decisive determinant. Even when the devolution is somewhat significant, the traditional elites may usurp and use the powers at the detriment of the common people and the very enfranchisement may face resistance from the ruling leadership of the local governments (as in West Bengal, Ghatak et al., 2002). Above all, the political motive behind the decentralisation drive including the design, the perception of the functionaries, the nature of engagement of the stakeholders and the socio-political ethos and practices, condition the performance and outcome of the decentralised units.

Against the overall backdrop, this study intended to explore the role of Gram Sabha and Gram Sansad in terms of the perception of the member-villagers, the participation of villagers in the deliberation of meetings, the nature of political machination in controlling the public participation, if any and the influence of these institutions over the decisions and activities of the Gram Panchayat. Another objective was to review the rationale behind the establishment of the Gram Unnayan Samity—another institution introduced at the Gram Sansad level by the 2003 amendment—and to assess how it entrenched people-centric governance. Succinctly, this study sought to evaluate and ascertain the public character and to peek into the prospect of the Gram Sabha, Gram Sansad and Gram Unnayan Samity as the governing institutions of the villagers.[18]

One noteworthy feature of the study is that all the structures that have subsequently been woven around GS—Gram Sabha and Gram Sansad and Gram Unnayan Samity (GUS)—have been covered. The primary survey for the study covers one Gram Sabha, two phases of Gram Sansads and 12 Gram Unnayan Samity meetings (wherever held) within each sample GP for the year 2007–08. Moreover, the secondary materials, to the extent available and relevant, have also been used for the exposition.

Necessary information and data have been collected mainly from three sources:

(i) Intensive interview based on pre-tested questionnaire—many with open ended responses—and informal yet informed discussion with two distinct categories of people: the general villager that is those people who are members of village assemblies and not officially attached to panchayat institutions or those people who have substantial stakes in the functioning of those assemblies. Another set was the elected GP members who are directly involved in Sansad and Gram Unnayan Samity activities.

(ii) All the information pertaining to public attendance, resolutions adopted and action plans prepared have been collected from the records maintained at GP office. It may, however, be noted that the access to records was denied by some GPs. Only after repeated persuasion, access could be gained somewhere, but not everywhere. One reason, revealed by informal sources, was that those GPs did not have well maintained records relating to the date, time, attendance of people in meetings and resolutions adopted. The secondary sources include published commentaries, reports dealing with GS meetings. Also the information uploaded in the website, particularly of Department of Panchayat, Government of India, helped considerably.

(iii) To get first hand information and understand what transpires in Sabha, Sansad meetings, participant observation was attempted, of course to the extent feasible. In such cases, the conduct of meetings was recorded for the purpose of analysis and documentation.

For collecting primary and secondary data, information relating to various aspects of village assemblies, one purposive sampling was done. Five districts of West Bengal were first selected based on geographical location, socio-political differentiations and possible access to GP areas. Though it is not customary in the survey methodology to focus on the access aspect, our field experience gives increasing credence to the fact that access is one decisive factor that determines the nature and depth of the investigation. Suffice it to say, free and easy access is not always forthcoming in a politically surcharged village society and panchayat system. The political leadership in particular and villagers in general are suspicious about the entry, posing questions and seeking panchayat related information. Without satisfactory credential and prior clearance, access is not generally granted. Indiscriminate sampling and expectation of hugging the land forthwith is likely to land one 'ordinary investigator' in trouble, at least in completing the survey works in West Bengal.

Of the five districts, Cooch Behar is from the north-eastern part of West Bengal and it is predominantly inhabited by SC, ST people and backward in terms of infrastructure and economic conditions. Paschim Midnapur is from south-western part and this district also has a significant proportion of tribal population. The remaining 3 districts are from the middle part or 'heart' of West Bengal. Birbhum is one traditionally backward district. Bardhaman is partly industrialised and often touted as the 'rice bowl' of Bengal. Murshidabad has a higher proportion of Muslim population. Politically, Paschim Midnapur and Bardhaman are regarded as the 'red bastion'—dominated by left parties. Murshidabad is the only district having, till the 7th panchayat elections, significant presence of the opposition party (Congress).

From each of the five districts, only two GPs from one administrative block (Panchayat Samity) were selected as the final sample for the study. The rationale and underlying assumptions guiding such selection of GPs included the following:

(i) Each sample district has large enough geographical spread and socio-economic diversities. For the sake of uniformity, the sample GPs from each block should not be too disparate and heterogeneous in terms of population composition, agricultural conditions, occupational patterns, etc. Thus, two GPs from each district are from one administrative block.

(ii) It is already manifested that villagers residing near to urban centres and having gained urban exposure are less inclined and those living far-off from town areas are more prone to participate in GS meetings (as in Kerala and Goa). For identifying whether such geographical differentiation is also pronounced in West Bengal, one sample GP from each block was adjacent to and another was distant from sub-divisional town.

(iii) Perhaps the more striking feature of West Bengal panchayat system is that it has overt political orientation, which is why panchayats in West Bengal are regarded as 'political' or 'red' panchayat. Political parties not only openly and invariably participate in elections but they also run panchayats with "party political objectives". Politics has pervaded every nook and corner of village society and villagers clearly are politically polarised. As the left (CPM, CPI, FB, RSP,) and non-left parties (Congress, TMC, BJP)[19] have divergent ideology, party organisation and style of functioning, the political party is likely to be one independent variable in influencing the role performance of Sansad and Sabha members. Therefore, from within every block, one sample GP was under the control of left parties and another (whenever existed)[20] was under the control of non-left party

The locale of the study is indeed unique. A peek into the working of village assemblies in West Bengal seems absorbing because the Panchayat system in the state has few exclusive features and if the positive claims about panchayats in the state are believed, many optimism and postulations concerning GS can come into fruition in this state.

West Bengal is the only state where PRIs have longer uninterrupted stint. The undulating graph reaching ups and downs in quick succession or causing breaks might have been the norms elsewhere, but in the state the political regime or CPM[21] has sustained panchayats since 1978. As democratic decentralisation involves system change, an extended period is required for gelling and fostering the new institutions and practices. Panchayats in West Bengal have got such an opportunity and they are in a relatively stronger position to actualise many goals of democratic decentralisation.

Panchayats in West Bengal have purportedly evolved into dynamic, vibrant and robust popular institutions. The capture of political power by the marginal and poor groups has reshaped the structure and practices of panchayat power. The rural masses have consequently got real involvement, interest and stake in panchayats.[22] Villagers' power over local affairs has increased, their knowledge-base has expanded and they are now so empowered that they are ready to interfere in order to defend their rights (Lieten, 2003: 225). As a result, panchayat meetings are regularly held, discussion is open, decision-making is need based, corruption and leakage in fund utilisation is minimum.[23] The genuine and comprehensive decentralisation benefiting the rural poor substantially[24] is advanced as the basic reason explaining the continuous electoral renewal of the Left Front government.[25]

The supposed objective conditions, representative character and pro-poor commitment of the panchayat leadership will have profound ramifications for the nature and working of the village assemblies in West Bengal. Based on the new idioms of panchayat politics like equity, involvement, assertiveness, responsiveness, need-based planning and equitable distribution of developmental benefits, the village assemblies in the state can expectedly be streaming and kicking.

Notes and References

1. "History affords no example of a highly underdeveloped country that has established a durable and effective political democracy. Full democracy has only been successfully tried out at an advanced stage of economic development .... The initial hopes that the newly independent nations of South Asia could establish full democracies or sustain them were not well founded .... Indian democracy has proved remarkably stable, but it is largely the stability of stagnation, certainly in regard to the needed reforms of the country's rigidly inegalitarian structure" (Myrdal, Gunnar (1972: 124–25), *Asian Drama*, New York: Penguin Books.)
2. In 14th Lok Sabha, 125 MPs had criminal cases against them, like murder, rape, extortion, dacoity, kidnapping, etc., for which they could have been imprisoned for at least 2 years. The background study by the Public Affairs Centre, Bangalore, revealed that each MP had, on average, an asset value of ₹ 1.66 crore and there was a close relation between asset, education and criminal charge. MPs with graduation or higher degree had asset value of ₹ 1.37 crore and 21 per cent of them had criminal antecedent. Those having lower education had ₹ 1.93 crore asset value and 30 per cent of them faced criminal charges. Few

MPs were found directly involved in human trafficking. Some took cash for raising query in parliament, for which 10 MPs were once expelled. In the 15th Lok Sabha (2009), a total of 150 MPs had criminal background, an increase of 7 percentage points.

3. Amendments to the Salaries and Allowances of Members of Parliament Act, 1954 are constantly enhancing their salaries, etc. 2010 Amendment Bill proposes ₹ 1.3 lakh as salary, allowance, office expense and secretarial service per month. This is besides daily allowances, free accommodation, telephones, travels and medical treatment. They will now get a pension of ₹ 21.8 lakh per annum, even if the legislature works for a single day after election.

   Some legal questions are: (i) can anyone receive allowances for no additional work but for the same work for which he is paid salary, (ii) Art. 106 of the constitution provides for salary and allowance but not for pension, (iii) as MPs receive salary for the whole year and as they pursue profession or hold office of profit, they tend to draw double salaries when employed and double pensions when retired.
4. Villoro, Luis (1998: 97), 'Which Democracy?', in *Democracy: Its Principles and Achievement*, Geneva: Inter-Parliamentary Union, 95–103.
5. The liberal representative model is fraught with many inconsistencies. If the majority is stable, the minority party gets lost. In case the majority is unstable, there is strong incentive for forming or changing alliance opportunistically. The situation turns murkier in a multicultural society and in a political system where parties are centred on charismatic personalities and loyal followers. Moreover, this form of government has the potential to distort the will of the majority as amplified by Ostrogorski paradox.
6. Consider few facts. About 52 per cent of total electorate, on an average, vote in general elections, thus a considerable portion does not register its consent. BJP and Congress party that headed coalition governments at the centre during 1999 and 2004 received respectively only 24 per cent and 26.5 per cent of total votes polled. Despite such minuscule support they ruled

the country as if representing the collective wishes of the Indian people.

7. Poverty is a relative concept and its measurement is debatable. India follows a calorie based approach for measuring the extent of poverty. A strong correlation between malnutrition and other notions of poverty (low income) is assumed, ignoring in the process expenditure on health, education, etc. Here two divergent methodologies are: uniform recall period and mixed recall period.
8. Dreze and Deaton, 2009. 'Food and Nutrition in India: Facts and Interpretation', *Economic & Political Weekly,* February 14. The World Bank (2009: 48, *Global Economic Prospect: Commodities at the Crossroads*, Washington) estimates that one quarter (313 million) of Indian people will be living in 2015 on less than $1.25 a day—a new poverty line for extreme poverty. The International Food Policy Research Institute in its Global Hunger Index, 2008, has placed India at 68th rank and warned against alarming extent of hunger in 12 Indian states. All these indicate that elections may have produced governments but the basic necessities of the greater number remain unfulfilled.
9. A turnout of about 40 per cent electorate in local government elections is generally accepted as satisfactory. Yet, such a benchmark is not always maintained. Less than 25 per cent voters—somewhere below 15 per cent—bothered to cast vote during 1999 local government elections in the United Kingdom (Norton, Philip (2001: 200), *The British Polity,* New York: Longman.)
10. Institutional reforms to bolster people's participation have sparked lively debate. The empirical measurement of participation is facing methodological critique—what should be the basis for a comparative assessment. From another perspective, low voting rate is believed to reflect the satisfaction of the electorate. Conversely, high turnout may indicate the collapse of the consensus (Lipset, S. (190: 101), *Political Man*, New York: Doubleday). Increased participation might also threaten the working of democracy because non-voting is pronounced among the ignorant sections.

11. Within deepening democracy strand there are at least four different, though not mutually exclusive approaches. Civil society's role is seen as an autonomous, countervailing power against the state. Participatory governance emphasises on direct involvement of citizens in the democratic process and core affairs of the sate. In deliberative democracy, citizens are to address public problems by deliberating how best to solve those. Empowered participatory governance seeks to deepen the ways in which people's participation influences public policy and solution of problems through dialogue and group choice.
12. Other terminologies have also been used to convey similar meaning and focus. Blair (2000) preferred 'democratic local governments' and UNDP (2002) opted for 'decentralising democratically'.
13. The term democratisation has recently appeared in the discourse of democracy. It refers to either a process through which one undemocratic political system tries to embrace democracy or as a continuum leading to strengthening and consolidating democracy. Anyway, democratisation is process oriented, represents evolutionary development and its content is relative and contextual, particularly in respect to the accountability to the people.
14. The recent wave of decentralisation is regarded as democratic and right based. Democratic decentralisation occurs when power and resources are transferred to authority representative of, and accountable to, local people. It aims to increase public participation in decision-making and to offer greater benefits than the erstwhile decentralisation endeavours. Democratic decentralisation is an institutionalised form of participatory approach (Ribot, 2004: 8).
15. The local government was intended to: (i) achieve fuller political and economic integration, (ii) establish reliable and continuous information network in the countryside (iii) recruit and co-opt intermediate and affluent classes for acting in concert with the government, (iv) bail out provincial governments from financial crisis by making local institutions responsible for maintaining public services and establishing infrastructure out of non-tax revenue (Bandyopadhyay, Ghosh and Ghosh (2007: 55–56), 'Dependency Versus Autonomy:

The Identity Crisis of Indian's Panchayats', in Mahanty, Baun, Ma and Mathew, eds, *Grassroots Democracy in India and China*, New Delhi: Sage)

16. Ward Sabha, to be based on each GP ward, will meet twice a year and will generate proposals, fix priority and select location of development scheme, identify beneficiaries (including verification of eligibility), assist scheme implementation and promote awareness and unity. Gram Sabha, meeting at least once in every two month, will identify, approve the socio-economic development programmes and select beneficiaries out of those approved by Ward Sabha, certify proper utilisation of fund, seek clarification, exercise social audit and own and manage resources and utilities. This Model Act seeks to provide a reference point for future panchayat laws of the state governments.
17. To one insistence, GS can help preventing environmental catastrophe by promoting land improvement, plantation, organic farming, clean development mechanism, conserving bio-diversity and motivating people to keep earth cool and green. Somkuwar, Awanish, 2009. 'Gram Sabha: Response to Climate Change', *The India Post*, 30 November.
18. Given the conceptual conundrum, how Gram Sabha can be conceived could have been one important objective, but this study excludes such exposition, which can be found in Mandal, Amal, 2010. 'Gram Sabha and Grassroots Governance: Concept and Contour', in Ghosh, M. and Jana, A.K., eds, *Development and Disorder: The Crises of Governance in the North East and East of India*. New Delhi: South Asian Publishers. pp. 275–290.
19. CPM: Communist Party of India (Marxist); CPI: Communist Party of India; FB: All India Forward Block; RSP: Revolutionary Socialist Party; Congress: Indian National Congress; TMC: Trinamul Congress; BJP: Bharatiya Janata Party. In subsequent pages only the short forms of the parties have been used and those are without prefixing 'the'.
20. As in Paschim Midnapur and Bardhaman, not a single GP within the sample block was under the control of non-left parties.

21. The Left Front government consists technically of many left parties. But CPM is the dominant one that has all through won far more seats in state assembly and panchayats and it has almost unilaterally controlled public policies. Also the ideological distinctiveness and unified party organisation make CPM different from other left parties. Because of meagre seat share, smaller left front partners do not have considerable influence and on many occasions they had to swallow the directives of CPM. Moreover, the left parties have consistently fought against each other in panchayat elections. Even when 'junior' partners controlled few panchayats, CPM did not allow them free reign, as some ethnographic studies point out (Roy, D. and Banerjee, 2006. 'Left Front's Electoral Victory in West Bengal'. *Economic & Political Weekly*, 7 October, 4251–4256; Dasgupta, 2009). In practical terms, Left Front and CPM can be used interchangeably.
22. For recent official averments see *Thirty Years of Left Front Government in West Bengal: Issues and Reflection*, 2007. Kolkata: Department of Information and Cultural Affairs, Government of West Bengal; Misra, Suryakanta, 2008. 'Thirty Years of Panchayat: The Road Traversed'. *People's Democracy*, 32(18), 32 (20).
23. Bardhan and Mookerjee, 2004. 'Poverty Alleviation Efforts of Panchayats in West Bengal'. *Economic & Political Weekly*. 28 February; Gazdar and Sengupta, 1997. 'Agrarian Politics and Rural Development in West Bengal', in Dreze and Sen, eds, *Indian Development—Select Regional Perspective*. New Delhi: Oxford University Press; Crook and Sverrisson. 1999.
24. One typical claim is that panchayats are responsive to the needs of the rural poor and people regard panchayat as their own institution. "Even the non-beneficiaries who have the reasons to be hostile to the panchayat for their not having derived any benefits, hold the panchayat in high esteem" (Pramanik, N. and Datta, P., (1994: 64). *Panchayats and People: West Bengal Experiment*. Calcutta (Kolkata): Sarat Book House.)
25. Contrary to such assertion, the (West Bengal) State Committee of CPM has recently conceded that the drubbing of CPM in the 15th general elections was due to the consolidation of anti-left votes following the tie-up of Congress and TMC as a result of

Left parties' withdrawal of support to UPA government at the centre on the issue of Indo-USA Nuclear deal. The State Committee noted that CPM's electoral success in West Bengal largely depended on the division of anti-left votes engineered by dividing wedge principally between Congress and TMC. LF's limited success in 2008 panchayat elections was admittedly due to unofficial alliance between Congress and TMC, hastened by the aggressive pitch for and highhandedness in farm land acquisition. The state committee reportedly decided on wooing Congress party back (Source: *The Statesman*, 13 June, 2009, page 1). Perhaps as a corollary to such assessment, Jyoti Basu, former Chief Minister, issued one open letter (dated 1.11.2009) during November, 2009 Lok Sabha elections requesting Congress party supporters to cast votes in favour of left candidates.

2

Evolution and Efficacy of Gram Sabha

The Gram Sabha is, in generic sense, the institutional space opened at the Gram Panchayat level. This assembly of villagers is for periodic interaction between the electorate and elected GP members. This umbrella organisation offers opportunity to all the electorate irrespective of any conceivable caste/class divides, to discuss community concerns, to influence decision-making process of GP including resource allocation and programme design, to insert their perceived priorities in village development plan, to enforce accountability of GP members and to reinforce democratic governance. GS can enable the marginal and vulnerable sections to assert themselves, fight against their browbeating by the dominant caste/class and to seek out solution to their exclusive problems. With the maturity of the institution and growing confidence of the villagers, GS is likely to script a brand new village visage.

GS is one unique institution. Unlike any other Indian political stratum where people's involvement begins and ends with electing their representatives as and when the opportunity comes, GS allows direct participation of people and exercise of power without any recourse to the representatives. By enabling direct participation and community decision-making, GS is likely to offer voice to the voiceless people and to checkmate the degeneration of the "power to the people" into "power to the powerful". GS can restore power to the people to whom it ought to but does not ordinarily belong.

The crucial and pivotal role that local democracy usually plays is likely to come to fruition at the parlance of GS. Dreze and Sen (2002: 359)[1] inform that local democracy provides the enabling means of participation in the wider democratic system; it is the potent force that fosters social change and transforms unequal relations of almost every kind. From the service delivery perspective, local democracy plays a critical role in enforcing responsiveness to the popular demands and in improving the quality of programmes. Being easily accessible particularly to the disadvantaged groups and having direct impact on people's lives, participation in local democracy has many intrinsic values.

However, democracy has three distinct yet interrelated dimensions: ideal, institution and process. While the ideals are the cherished objectives and values by themselves, the institutional arrangement is for achieving the ideals. How the institutions so established are working or evolving is the part of the democratic process and it is more critical because mere institutions however innovative or comprehensive, may not always be enough especially in the Indian context. The process is context dependent and circumstance specific. The expanse of institution and its actual working are contingent upon socio-economic and political factors. It is well known that the social inequities act as the barriers that hold up the process of local democracy, as in the sphere of panchayats. What is little known is the fact that political motive, response, incentive structure and the democratic culture—encouraging active participation and open deliberation on public issues—also play crucial role in shaping and directing the local democratic process.

How the institutional space created through GS is actualising the ostensible goal of local democracy and governance requires critical reflection and appreciation. However, one needs to tread cautiously because India has too much of wrong kinds of democracy and not enough of right kind (Kohli, 1992: x). The emphasis has all along been on basing Indian democracy on the willing consent of people and complying with the public view on the problems and their solutions but the reality check tells a different story. Moreover, the establishment of panchayats has been impelled less by the democratic motives and more by the administrative compulsions like stopping leakage in development expenditure, quick response to problems and they are yet to emerge as self-governing institution shaking off their development agency image.

The focus of this chapter is on the evolution of the institution and the role performance of GS in West Bengal in particular and other Indian states in general. The all-India exposition is intended to put West Bengal scenario in broader perspective. In the subsequent analysis two analytical categories have been employed. GS prevalent during the historic period since independence to 1992 is regarded as pre-amendment vintage and its reincarnation consequent upon 73rd Constitutional Amendment is called post-amendment form. In the post-amendment era GS is of two kinds—one special category having different legal layout is exclusively for the 5th scheduled areas and another general breed applicable to all non-scheduled region, that is everywhere except in the 5th and 6th scheduled areas as earmarked in the Indian Constitution itself. Except for a brief description of its nature, the special category GS has been excluded from the delineation because it is one exclusive class applicable to specified areas and this breed is not obtainable in West Bengal.

Evolution of the Legal Layout

When panchayats were being introduced following Balawantrai Mehta Committee recommendations, many state panchayat legislations incorporated provisions for GS. As to its composition, two contrasting modes were perceptible—GS consisted of either all adult members in GP area (Bihar, Mysore, Rajasthan) or all registered electorate. In some states it was coterminous with the revenue village and somewhere for a group of villages (Assam, Gujarat, Madhya Pradesh, Punjab, Uttar Pradesh, Rajasthan, Jammu & Kashmir). Though the size varied from 250 to 5,000, the average number of members comprising one GS was around 300 (Maddick, 1970: 70). Its main functions extended to consideration of the annual GP statement of audit, review of progress of works, drawing up of village development plan for the coming year, consideration/approval of annual budget (GoI, 1963: 7; Maddick, 1970: 74). Orissa had one Palli Sabha in every village within the multi-village GP and it could suggest imposition of enhanced labour tax on able-bodied men and women in the area concerned (Maddick, 1970: 75).

During the pre-amendment period the conception of GS was disparate. In some states, as in West Bengal, GS was conceived more like a legislature electing directly from among themselves all members of the Gram Panchayat as one responsible executive organ. In other states GS was like one village assembly empowered to consider activity reports of GP.

Till the promulgation of 73rd Amendment, there was no serious attempt to establish a strong GS, except in Karnataka (1985) and West Bengal (1992). GS did not find favour with the central level committees constituted to suggest how to strengthen or revitalise panchayats. Balawantrai Mehta Committee (1957) was more obsessed with Block level panchayat and it had misgivings on even the potential of GP. Diwankar Committee (GoI, 1963) favoured graduation, spontaneity and natural (not legal) growth of GS, not in isolation but in organic unity with panchayat system. Ashok Mehta Committee (1978) even after recognising its huge importance was silent on legal entitlement of GS.[2]

During the period when panchayats in general were in dilapidated condition and GS was being abandoned in subsequent state panchayat acts (as in West Bengal and Madhya Pradesh) Karnataka took one initiative establishing robust type of GS, more akin to post-amendment dispensation. Karnataka

Zilla Parishad, Taluka Panchayat Samity, Mandal Panchayat and Nyaya Panchayat Act, 1983 ordained GS in every revenue village consisting of all persons registered in the electoral roll of Zilla Parishad. GS was to prepare and promote development schemes of the village, organise sanitation and drainage schemes, mobilise voluntary labour, collect contribution in kind or cash for community welfare programme and it was to assist Mandal Panchayat in programme implementation. GS also could select beneficiaries and constitute Land Army whose members would be employed under the ongoing development schemes. The recommendation of GS had to be considered by Mandal and Zilla panchayat.

The 73rd Amendment Act, 1992 is one epoch in the history of Panchayati Raj. This landmark act constitutionalises three tier panchayat structures and ordains certain basic features like certainty, continuity and strength to panchayat. This central act has enjoined the institution of GS, though briefly, if not obliquely. Consequent upon the 73rd Amendment, the state governments have provided for institution of GS in their respective panchayat acts where the scope and functions along with the methodology of the working have been outlined. But the scope, functions and the dispensation vary from one state to another. However, GS has primarily been conceived as one primary body of village panchayat for facilitating direct participation of people. GS has been set to serve as an assembly of the villagers and to foster people's participation in the panchayat process.

Few commentators are upbeat in asserting that 73rd Amendment has mandated GS and states have followed the constitutional directive. How far such a contention is tenable remains unclear. In fact, the 73rd Amendment Act refers to GS only twice: in the part of definitions and at the outset of the detailed provisions. GS has been defined as "the body consisting of persons registered in electoral rolls relating to a village comprised within the area of a panchayat at the village level". Art. 243(A) thereafter provides: GS "may exercise such powers and perform such functions at the village level as the legislature of a state may by law provide", thus, this provision effectively allows state legislature to work on GS according to their perception or expediency. Moreover, indicative is the use of the term "may", which constitutionally implies non-binding connotation. Noteworthy is the use of "shall" for every other facets of panchayats (GP, PS, ZP, Election Commission, Finance Commission, etc.). Notwithstanding the follow-up action of states, 73rd Amendment is somewhat ambivalent on GS and this is perhaps due to rather "horrible" working experience and reluctance of erstwhile committees to grant legal status to GS.

Before the delineation of the overall structure, powers and functions of GS during post-amendment period few qualifications are in order: (i) Since 1996, GS has got two distinct breeds. One special category with elevated constitutional status and extraordinary powers is applicable only for the 5th scheduled areas and another with relatively subdued status and power is for non-scheduled or general areas. (ii) Regarding composition, GS lacks homogeneity. Somewhere it is established for the entire territorial area of a GP, or regarded as one composite unit and in some other states it has two separate tiers, additional one being at the ward (constituency) level of a GP. Where GS has two tiers, the nature of powers, functions and the relationship between the two tiers are divergent and complicated. Even when GS is one composite unit the situation is far from infallible—the agenda items of the meetings to be held in a year are different across the board. (iii) Regarding powers and functions of GS unequivocal elaboration is one tricky task. The statutory provisions are undergoing frequent changes, often through administrative rules, which are difficult to trace or take note of. While assigning powers and functions the state panchayat acts have used terminologies/wordings that have conflicting connotations defying generalisation. For instance, as regards GP budget, GS is to consider or discuss or approve or pass it. The use of such phrases like subjects to be placed before GS for consideration, for approval, for making recommendation and suggestion tends also to erode the powers and credibility of GS.

Gram Sabha under PESA

Art. 243(M) of the 73rd Amendment barred the extension of the envisaged panchayat system to the 5th scheduled areas because it was considered inappropriate in the context of homogeneous character of tribes and the existence of traditional self-governing institutions in the tribal society. One separate enactment—Panchayat (Extension to the Scheduled Areas) Act, 1996 (PESA) (effective from 24 December, 1996)—has extended panchayat system to the scheduled (tribal) areas.[3] Unlike the 73rd Amendment, the PESA has itself detailed the composition, powers and functions of GS.

The PESA, in short, is one unprecedented enactment that gives radical self-governing powers to the tribal communities. Under it, GS is believed to have been based on few crucial axes. The basic unit is the organic self-governing community. The habitation is the natural unit of the community whose adult members constitute GS. The PESA makes a paradigm shift in the sense that every GS shall be competent—and not to be empowered by endowment of powers by states legislation as is required for the general category—to safeguard and preserve the traditions and customs of the tribal people, their cultural identity, community resources and customary mode of dispute resolution. Instead of endowment that may or may not come, GS under the PESA shall be authorised and competent to exercise powers and to uphold the community interests. Here the relationship between GP and GS is like executive and legislature. GS will see and certify fund utilisation and will be competent to monitor all state institutions within its jurisdiction (school, health centre). GS will have the right to be consulted on acquisition of or access to land and land related resources. Prior approval of GS will be necessary before granting licence or lease for minor mineral or their exploration. Above all, GS will be supreme as its powers cannot be usurped by any other higher panchayat tier.

However, the radical promise of the PESA and the pivotal role of GS therein still remains on paper only. The PESA is yet to be mainstreamed in the state policies as most states are lukewarm in making conformity laws and rules, for which GS tends to be languishing as an advisory body. Somewhere, the states have deconstructed PESA through legal contortions, thus reducing the progressive legislation to a nullity. State laws compound the confusion by authorising either panchayat, or GS or panchayat at appropriate level to perform functions earmarked in PESA. By and large, the prospect of a face-to-face and powerful GS has so far been precluded by the state laws and rules.[4]

Post-Amendment Period

While the special category GS enjoys constitutional status and decisive powers and Madhya Pradesh has extended such powers and functions to all GSs within the state, for the general category GS sharp variations regarding the structure, powers, functions and role are observable. And this is understandable because states, taking the discretion and leeway offered by the 73rd Amendment, have gone in their dissimilar ways. However, the general category GS has primarily been conceived as the village assembly expected to enlist and foster direct participation of people in the affairs of GP.

One direct and positive impact of 73rd Amendment is on the composition of GS. Regarding membership, the state panchayat acts envisage that all the electorate registered in the assembly electoral roll will be the member of GS. This is in accordance with the definition of the central act and conforms to the democratic principle and the mode seems appropriate as it integrates GS with the overall structure of Indian democracy.

Together with one composite unit at GP level, many states have gone for one additional unit at ward level. The ideal size of GS has been one ticklish issue since earlier times. One composite unit can work well as long as the geographical spread and population size are small and manageable. Where GP is large enough (as in West Bengal, Kerala, Assam) the relationship between people and GP members becomes distant, their partnership tends to weaken, problems of smaller habitation get overlooked, GP may assume the role of a superior bureaucratic structure, and the concept of subsidiary gets diluted. Any effort to hasten solution by reducing the size of GP itself is likely to weaken the capacity and administrative viability and to debase the support structure and resource base of GP, as the 2nd Administrative Reform Commission (2007) rightly perceived. Accordingly, few committees proposed creation of two-tier GS.[5] The two-tier structure is likely to ensure closer proximity with villagers, facilitate participation of people, retain the administrative viability of GP and will enable preparation of realistic development plan.[6]

Table 2.1

Synoptic Profile of Gram Sabha in General (Non-Scheduled) Areas (as on 2006)

Gram Sabha constituted at Ward level	*States*
	Dadra & Nagar Haveli, Goa (only Ward Committee), Himachal Pradesh, Jharkhand (for Scheduled Area), Karnataka, Kerala (only at Ward level), Orissa, Rajasthan, Sikkim, Tripura, West Bengal.
Meetings	
1. Twice a year	Andhra Pradesh, Haryana (3 times), Karnataka, Lakshadweep, Manipur, Orissa, Rajasthan, Sikkim, Uttar Pradesh, Uttarakhand, West Bengal,
2. 4 times a year	Assam, Maharashtra (6 times), Chhattisgarh, Gujarat, Jharkhand, Kerala, Tamil Nadu, Madhya Pradesh, Goa, Dadra & Nagar Haveli.
3. Provision for requisition meeting	Haryana, Himachal Pradesh, Kerala, Madhya Pradesh, Punjab, Rajasthan, Uttar Pradesh.
4. Fixed meeting date	Andhra Pradesh, Assam, Bihar, Goa, Gujarat (1st Sunday of month), Madhya Pradesh, Orissa, Tamil Nadu.
Quorum	
1. More than 10 per cent	Himachal Pradesh, Jharkhand, Maharashtra, Punjab, Sikkim, Tripura (for Sansad), Uttarakhand,

Cont'd...

...Cont'd

2. Just 10 per cent	Arunachal Pradesh, Assam, Bihar Chhattisgarh, Goa, Gujarat, Karnataka, Kerala, Lakshadweep, Madhya Pradesh, Manipur, Orissa, Rajasthan, Tamil Nadu, West Bengal.
3. Quorum scaled down subsequently	Assam, Madhya Pradesh, Tamil Nadu, Uttar Pradesh,
4. No quorum for adjourned meeting	Bihar, Goa, Himachal Pradesh (1/2 less), Jharkhand, Manipur, Orissa, Punjab (1/2 less), Uttar Pradesh, West Bengal
Provision for Vigilance Committee	Bihar, Goa, Gujarat, Himachal Pradesh, Jammu & Kashmir (only Monitoring Committee), Jharkhand, Manipur, Rajasthan.
Functions	
1. Approval of development plan of GP	Assam, Bihar, Chhattisgarh, Goa, Gujarat, Himachal Pradesh, Jammu & Kashmir, Jharkhand, Karnataka, Kerala, Lakshadweep, Madhya Pradesh, Maharashtra, Manipur, Orissa, Punjab, Rajasthan, Tamil Nadu, Tripura, Uttar Pradesh,
2. Examine/review of development works (including quality)	Andhra Pradesh, Assam, Bihar Gujarat, Karnataka, Madhya Pradesh, Punjab, Rajasthan, Sikkim, West Bengal.
3. Consider/approve GP Budget	Andhra Pradesh, Arunachal Pradesh, Chhattisgarh, Gujarat, Haryana, Jharkhand, Karnataka, Kerala, Madhya Pradesh, Manipur, Orissa, Punjab, Tamil Nadu, Tripura, Uttarakhand, West Bengal.
4. Consider annual statement of GP, audit report, etc.	Andhra Pradesh, Assam, Bihar Goa, Gujarat, Himachal Pradesh, Jharkhand, Karnataka, Kerala, Madhya Pradesh, Manipur, Punjab, Sikkim, Tamil Nadu, Tripura, Uttar Pradesh, West Bengal
5. Select/approve beneficiary	Andhra Pradesh, Arunachal Pradesh, Assam, Bihar Chhattisgarh, Goa, Gujarat, Himachal Pradesh, Jammu & Kashmir, Jharkhand, Karnataka, Kerala, Madhya Pradesh, Maharashtra, Manipur, Orissa, Punjab, Rajasthan, Sikkim, Tamil Nadu, Tripura, Uttarakhand, Uttar Pradesh, West Bengal.

Cont'd...

...Cont'd

6.	Consider proposal for fresh taxation/enhancement of rate	Andhra Pradesh, Goa, Orissa, Sikkim.
7.	Placement of receipt, expenditure, voucher of all purchase, salary of PR staff, measurement work, utilisation of allocated fund	Assam, Tamil Nadu
8.	Seek clarification from GP President/member about activity/scheme/programme	Bihar, Goa (right to obtain information), Himachal Pradesh, Kerala (right to know fund allocation/utilisation), Punjab, Rajasthan
9.	Issue of utilisation/completion certificate for work undertaken in area concerned	Goa, Himachal Pradesh, Jharkhand, Karnataka, Madhya Pradesh, Orissa, Rajasthan (from Ward Sabha), Sikkim (from Vigilance Committee).
10.	Disciplinary control over government, semi-government/PR employee working in area concerned	Himachal Pradesh, (inquire and report misconduct against officials like constable, peon, chowkidar, forest guard, GP Secretary), Madhya Pradesh, Maharashtra, Manipur.
11.	Conduct social audit/monitor GP functionary	Karnataka, Maharashtra, Sikkim

Regarding GS meetings, relatively improved position is discernable in the state acts. Two ordinary meetings every year is the general norm, only a few state acts envisage 3 or more meetings. More and more meetings may be useful as these will ensure continuous interaction with the people and impel GP to follow the recommendations of GS. But this can equally be counterproductive if GP does not get reasonable time to carry out earlier recommendations of GS. And there is a provision in few state acts for requisition and extraordinary meeting. Recent trends testify that many states are favouring fixed dates (mostly identical national holidays) for GS meetings. One advantage of such preordained dates is that people are well aware exactly when such meetings will be held and GP will have no scope for dithering such meetings.

Failure to hold stipulated GS meetings is legally unacceptable. If GP President fails to convene a meeting, the Executive Officer of Panchayat Samity (in Bihar), the Inspector of Panchayat (in Tamil Nadu) or Block Development Officer (in Goa) will convene such a meeting. And this will be after expelling GP President for defaulting in performing the statutory duty. In Kerala, if the ward member of GP (who is the convenor of GS) fails to convene GS meeting on two successive occasions s/he will cease to hold office (u/s 35).[7] If GP president or Vice President in Maharashtra fails to convene a meeting without showing sufficient justification s/he will be disqualified. However, the sting gets considerably diluted when it is provided that the District Collector will finally decide whether the reason(s) advanced for not holding such a meeting is acceptable or not. GP President will automatically cease to hold office from the date on which the 2nd meeting of GS is to be held (in Haryana, u/s 11(2) or from the last day of the month on which the 2nd meeting is to be held (in Punjab, u/s 5(3). However, the Directorate of Panchayat (in Punjab) can reinstate the President if he is convinced that the grounds for withholding such a meeting are compelling.

Most state acts prescribe a fixed quorum for GS meeting, without which the meeting will stand adjourned. Some states initially ordained for more than 10 per cent presence of members. But in view of persistent problem of achieving such proportion, many states subsequently scaled down the quantum of quorum. The common mode at present is for a presence of at least 10 per cent of total members, without having any outer limit. Few states also entail additional conditions: presence of proportionate number of SC, ST and women.

Outright absence of quorum for the adjourned meeting in some states is one worrisome trend. If GS meeting does not attract requisite number of people, the effort should rather be to convince and mobilise more and more people. When, instead, adjourned meetings are allowed to be held without any requirement of quorum, the popular apathy will perpetuate and GP members may, given the general trend, be encouraged to prefer or induce adjourned meeting where they will be able to pass convenient resolutions without obtaining public consent or facing public opposition and such an eventuality may turn the entire institutional fabric of GS upside down. Goa has one strange provision. If quorum is not available after 15 minutes from the appointed time, the meeting shall be adjourned by half an hour and after that time the meeting shall be held without any quorum. Thus, without attending to the cause and taking any corrective course, absence of people has been formalised and important decisions can legally be taken without the consent of the villagers.

Powers and Functions

GS in most state acts is competent to examine GP's annual administrative report, budget proposal, audit and accounts report, review the ongoing scheme works and development activities, deliberate on and somewhere approve future development programmes, mobilise people's participation and promote social unity and harmony.

Considering the overall gamut, the power and functions of GS may broadly be typified into three categories:

(i) *Developmental functions* embrace approval of village plan for socio-economic development, GP budget and selection of individual beneficiaries on priority basis after laying down or following ordained principles, selection of development schemes/programmes including the location, consideration of tax proposal or enhancement of existing rates and rendering assistance in implementation of development programmes.

(ii) *Review/monitoring functions* include consideration or review of GP's (annual) activities, implementation process of development programmes either collectively or through sub-committee or vigilance committee, seeking or obtaining clarification/information about GP activities, income and expenditure, scrutinising GP's audit and accounts report and giving completion or utilisation certificate relating to programme or fund expended within GS areas.

(iii) *Community mobilisation functions* extend to securing community participation and its contribution to welfare activities as well as to scheme implementation, building awareness or undertaking sensitisation programmes, as on education, family welfare or social harmony.

Notwithstanding such broad categorisation, few special and exclusive features deserve mention. Many state panchayat acts chart out functions which are no less glossy, aspirational or ritualistic. Perhaps these have been appended without sufficient contemplation as to how those can be undertaken or performed by GS. For instance, GS is to (i) promote social integration, unity among all sections of people, (ii) mobilise voluntary labour, collect contribution in kind or cash for community welfare programmes, (iii) assist in implementation of development schemes, (iv) activate people towards community welfare programmes, (v) enhance general consciousness among people, vi) expand and secure youth and family welfare, abolition of dowry and social evils like corruption, (vii) help disabled and destitute, (viii) disseminate information relating to development and welfare, (ix) sustain parent-teacher association (x) report on incidence of calamity, epidemic, etc., (xi) collect socio-economic data, (xii) support GP in collection of tax, repayment of loan, environment cleanliness, (xiii) help in survey activities like Census, and (xiv) promote adult education.

Few almost identical and at the same time 'ambitious' functions are also in evidence. GS is empowered (as in Jharkhand, Madhya Pradesh) to construct and maintain village road, culvert, bridge, tank, well, pond, light on road, regulate entertainment show, control selling of meat, fruit and milk, build public utilities, maintain records relating to birth, death and marriage and preserve GP property, historical monument, etc.

Besides those 'ornamental' powers, many state acts entrust some sweeping powers to GS. In Sikkim and Haryana, GS is to maintain completion register for all development works to be undertaken by GP and other government departments. In Madhya Pradesh it can audit the expenditure up to rupees three lakh and can also remove panchayat *karmi*, recall GP President and other members after completion of 2½ years of tenure through secret ballot. In Manipur GP President or Vice President can be removed if a resolution expressing lack of confidence is passed by 2/3 majority of members present and voting. Prior approval of GS will be necessary for incurring any expenditure and land acquisition in Maharashtra. GS members in Kerala will have the right to know the rationale behind GP decisions concerning the ward areas. GS conducts social audit in Karnataka (known as panchayat *janabandi*). In some cases sub-committee, standing committee, monitoring committee or vigilance committee is to supervise the development works or to devise development plans.

Nevertheless, the most common and frequently used function is the selection of individual beneficiaries for various public development programmes, though the statutory provisions across states are somewhat at variance. In one extreme, the list of beneficiaries finalised by GS in order of ward-level priority cannot anyway be reversed by GP (as in Karnataka u/s 3(A) (C). On the other, if GS fails to identify the beneficiary, GP (in Manipur) or GP Secretary in consultation with GP President or BDO (in Assam), or the prescribed authority (in Sikkim) will select those. Despite being the habitual function and having the huge potential to prevent the perversion as patronage distribution, the moot question is how far GS is really suitable for this task and whether its members are actually selecting beneficiaries objectively and without (political/other) bias.

As to the recommendations, resolutions passed by GS meetings in conformity with the prescribed procedure, two contrasting trends manifest. The recommendations are somewhat binding on GP. As in Chhattisgarh, Jharkhand, Madhya Pradesh, Karnataka, Goa and Uttar Pradesh, GP is mandated to follow and implement those so far as these are in conformity with the rules, regulation in force at the time. In Karnataka, for instance, any panchayat tier and even state government will have no power to change GS resolution, which can only be returned for reconsideration or amendment if there is any defect or deficiency.

In another side of the spectrum, GP 'shall' duly consider GS recommendations. Kerala provides perhaps the more realistic provision. GP will ordinarily abide by GS resolutions; in case or if at any time GS resolutions cannot be followed or implemented, the President of GP is obliged to report the incidence and elaborate the reason thereof (u/s 3(6).

In nutshell, therefore, the recommendations of GS are not entirely insignificant, though mere consideration by GP may not imply one enviable status. This is a vast improvement over the feeble status of GS during pre-amendment period. However, when GS decisions are somewhat binding on GP one gut issue is: will not the administrative efficiency of GP be then affected or compromised—one conventional argument earlier used against conferment of statutory powers to GS.

Operation of Gram Sabha in Indian States

For any institution the exercise of powers and performance of the envisaged role are more critical than the formal design and legal endowment. Ironically, during the entire pre-amendment period, GS fumbled to perform its designated role. What the research and other reports reveal is that GS had not been functioning to the desired extent; it failed to fulfil even a modicum of the prescribed functions and it did exist only notionally.

Regarding what happened in GS meeting and its outcome during pre-amendment era, disconcerting dimensions unfolded. Very few panchayats convened the prescribed number of meetings and that too under external pressure and without prior or proper notice. In many cases GP members were asked to come along with as many members as possible so as to meet the quorum. The notice of meeting, if given, failed to attract public attention. Meetings were held without pre-arranged plan, generally without agenda. People were ignorant about their rights and responsibilities as member of GS, they also could not differentiate between GS and GP (GoI, 1963: 12). The participation of people was rarely spontaneous or adequate. Quorum was continually a problem and the attendance rates were not only abysmally low but also often inflated (GoI, 1963; Jain, 1997; Mandar, 1999).[8] The presence of women was either negligible or nil, thus the representation of all sections of villagers was lacking. However, attendance could surge when some political leaders or high officials visited GP.

The traditional leaders, influential persons attended meetings for promoting personal or political interests rather than for discussing issues concerning planning and development. The meetings were also utilised by rival groups in criticising, ventilating, exposing or condemning some activities of GP members (Jain, 1997). Neither planning function nor GP budget was presented for discussion or approval. Most people were silent listeners. The proceedings were written without the knowledge of those who attended, they were not reported to GP/higher tier, nor was there follow-up action. However, there are few good examples (Jain, 1997: 561) where GS did act as the forum for free and close interaction between officials and non-officials, for consideration of people's hardship and difficulties, for appraising the works of GP and for disseminating latest information about public schemes.

Many inherent and socio-political constrictions such as lack of awareness of villagers, personal nature of village politics, lack of common venue, convenient time and proper communication for meetings, perceived futility of GS, aversion of GP members to face embarrassing questions and boycott of meeting by opposition parties and rival factions encumbered the meaningful role performance of GS (GoI, 1963: 13–14). Non-viable size and domination by GP chairperson and government officials were the other reasons (Maddick, 1970: 70).

Karnataka experience was no exception either. In most cases GS meeting was not convened or held.[9] Nor legal stipulation regarding the number of meetings per year was followed. As the 1983 act did not specify quorum, valid meeting could be held with just 7 members (Joshi and Shenoy, 1995: 197). Women's presence was subdued.[10] At the initial stage, meetings might have been held regularly but in due course the frequency, the number of villages where these were held and the attendance rate declined.[11] Majority of participants were predetermined beneficiaries for development schemes. Politicians used GS platform for building network, support base or rapport with villagers. No discussion on village development plan was held; somewhere it was reduced to making complaints or mud slinging.[12] Village level workers did not bother to attend for which discussion on village problems could not be made (Joshi and Shenoy, 1995: 197). Mandal Panchayat members were hesitant to face GS. And the arrangement for people's participation in decentralised planning process through GS became 'almost a defunct mechanism' (Bhargava and Raphael, 1994: 155).

One study covering post 1987 elections in Karnataka revealed how the questioning and confronting panchayat members could ultimately lead to the subversion of GS itself. The people initially felt empowered and they raised questions, lodged complaints and demanded better services, etc. Because of legal compulsion Mandal members had to tolerate such public criticism but they were not receptive to the open expression of public grievances, information demand and identification of beneficiaries in open meetings (Crook and Manor, 1998: 30). For some Mandal members GS meeting was humiliating, almost verging on the usurpation of their right to allocate benefits. Feeling frustrated and snubbed, the Mandal members began to abandon GS after one year or two, held unannounced meeting and selected beneficiaries from among their clientele.

Post-Amendment Phase

If during pre-amendment phase GS failed to spur villagers or it fumbled to evolve as one forum for reviewing the activities of GP or as one decision-making body, the overall situation continues to remain unsatisfactory even after statutory endowment of not so trivial powers and functions. GS is yet to fulfil its expected role as one deliberative body, as a mechanism for upholding accountability or as one participatory forum for governance (Johnson, 2003: 29; Alsop et al., 2000; Despande et al., 2002).

The attendance of people continues to be alarmingly low and unsatisfactory. In Madhya Pradesh and Andhra Pradesh, for instance, 69 per cent of total population in 63 villages did not attend a single meeting and only 7 per cent villagers attended regularly (Alsop et al., 2000: 17). One survey in north

Indian states (PRIA, 2001: 96) found that 80 per cent meetings lacked quorum. Even in the tribal society where there is a strong tradition of village assembly, smaller geographical spread and where the records of community actions are noteworthy, the achievement of quorum has been one persistent problem. The venue, time and agenda of meeting were kept secret (Fernandes, 2003: 2877; Joshep et al., 2000, Crook and Manor, 1998). Statutorily prescribed number of meetings was not convened—in 54 per cent cases not a single meeting was held in Andhra Pradesh.[13] For fulfilling legal norms, the attendance figures were manipulated by incorporating signatures of passer-by or collecting those from houses (Kumar, 2006).

Women's participation continues to suffer.[14] The timing of meeting—either at morning or noon—does not suit them. The politically surcharged ambience in the meeting discourages them. They are less aware about the powers and role of GS. The social inhibitions also stultify their involvement. When family males stay away for any reason, women feel it unfair or dangerous not to follow suit. One study found significant variations in participation between men and women in Madhya Pradesh but not in Kerala.[15] However, the difference between men and women in their ability to raise issues in the meeting was significant in Kerala but not in Tamil Nadu and Madhya Pradesh.

Two types of GS meeting were held, as in Karnataka. One was to identify the felt needs, demands of people. Another called at the behest of the Executive Officer, Block and Zilla Parishad was to pick out beneficiaries. The latter type, rather than the former, was more frequent, suggesting that officials played a predominant role in convening and conducting the meetings.[16] Similarly, if a government department intended ratification, approval of plan, selection of beneficiaries, auction of panchayat land, it used GS for its programme implementation (Nambiar, 2001: 3115). Thus, GS seems to be one agency to perform the superimposed agenda of government hierarchy.

In the meetings the GP President usually delivers a long lecture detailing inventory of development works undertaken by GP in the last year, a synoptic view of what GP will do in future. The presentation of administrative reports and statement of accounts is in such a manner that people cannot make head or tail and this is one important reason why such reports get approval without having any discussion or query. Moreover, government officials, wherever present, elaborate the objective and guidelines of the prevalent schemes so that people can comprehend and apply for those. All these take considerable time and leave little for the villagers to voice their views.

Even when the attendance rate is uniformly low, members tend to have only physical presence. Proactive participation in GS deliberation is exception rather than the rule. The recorded evidences from 290 GS meetings across Andhra Pradesh, Karnataka, Kerala and Tamil Nadu disclosed that each GS meeting lasted on average 84 minutes, a tiny section of villagers (around 84) participated. SC and women might have constituted 1/3 of total participants but they did not speak much in those meetings (Rao and Sanyal, 2009). Another study found that 45 per cent respondents did not utter a single word in GS meetings. The purpose of attendance was not to raise issues but to hand over application seeking assistance for themselves or family (Kumar, 2006: 223). Surely, those people did not get the assistance sought earlier. They again tried in GS forum expecting that they might find a favour in the open meeting.

People weigh opportunity cost of participation. They tend to skip meetings except when some direct benefits are in sight. In other words, eligible and prospective beneficiaries basically attend (Joseph and John, 2000: 269; Kumar, 2006) and they stake claim for available benefits. Some participants are also those persons interested in taking various developmental works on contract basis (PRIA, 2001).

People are not aware, and nobody has made them conscious of the fact that they have now got the power to influence and control the decision-making process of GP through meaningful participation in GS meetings. Such low awareness is mainly due to the (wrong) focus of GP on the material benefits to the poor rather than to strengthen local governance. People have been made to perceive and accept GS as a benefits distribution centre (John, 2007: 235). The distinct value is the participation for the benefits and not participation itself. Even GP members have blurred vision about GS (Mukarji and Bandyopadhyaya, 1993; Bhattacharya, 2002).

The legal compulsions concerning GS meeting have put GP members in a spot of bother and they have consequently devised tactics to subvert or stifle possible encroachment on their powers by the masses. When people try to put claims or select beneficiaries, GP members attempt to undermine or avoid this forum. The circulation of notice of meeting is withheld as the presence of large number of the people might upset the vested interest of members. Meetings are called on short notice so as to offset formation of opinion or stand. Meetings are also called on weekly market day to prevent a large congregation, thus allowing GP members to select their cronies as beneficiaries. GP members themselves disrupt meeting when uncomfortable questions are posed (Srivastava, 1999).

Attendance of people tends to rise when sensitive issues—politically or otherwise—are taken up for decision-making: for instance, merger of panchayat area with municipality (as in Goa, Fernandes, 2003: 2873), when collective village interests are at stake (like licence to DuPont or Coco Cola company) and when GP members rise above narrow political, sectional divide and take initiative, use personal influence and mobilise people.[17] Moreover, qualitative and quantitative participation petrifies when civil society organisations take active role in disseminating information, building awareness and mobilising people.[18]

Worth pondering is one assertion. The Andhra Pradesh government had pursued a policy that diluted the powers and authority of panchayat institutions. Its brand of "development populism" created many user committees as parallel bodies to which funds earmarked for panchayats were assigned. Mandal level officials did have active role in GS meetings which were used only as a means of selecting beneficiaries, announcing allocation for *Janmabhoomi* and food-for-work programme. Against such odds, participation of people in GS meeting was found substantially higher—73 per cent compared to 48 per cent in Madhya Pradesh. The apparent dichotomy is said to be due to the fact that unlike Madhya Pradesh, GS meetings in Andhra Pradesh had established one direct and predictable relations and those meetings had evolved as the alternative means where villagers could interact with the state, receive information about and gain access to formal state entitlements directly affecting their lives such as micro credit (Johnson et al., 2005: 954).

In Kerala and Madhya Pradesh

The working of GS in Kerala and Madhya Pradesh during post-amendment period deserves special mention because GSs therein rose to prominence, though for a brief period. The 2001 amendment in Madhya Pradesh impacted a paradigmatic shift in the principle of governance—from representative to direct democracy. GS under *Gram Swaraj*, got direct decision-making powers including finance; it could decide on almost anything befalling under the jurisdiction of GP. Monthly GS meeting and several standing committees comprising stakeholders and enjoying implementational responsibility could have really enthused people to come and use GS forum. Madhya Pradesh offered one opportunity to test the hypothesis that people's apathy to GS is due to insignificant powers of GS.

However, the gaps between the rhetoric surrounding 'direct democracy' and actual working of GS in Madhya Pradesh were too wide to ignore. The working experience was not quite heartening. GS might have received decision-making powers but its meetings had not been held every time and everywhere. People's attendance, in general was thin[19] and those meetings remained preoccupied with beneficiary selection. Though GS was to select members of the standing committees, the power was actually exercised by the *Sarpanchas* (GP President), often in collaboration with the line department officials whose programme was being implemented in the village. The selection of members of the standing committees was essentially a matter of compiling a list of names and submission of it to the department concerned.[20] Not only committee members were unaware about their membership, the committees themselves were powerless and ineffectual (Johnson et al., 2005: 954). Though *Gram Swaraj* was intended to clip the emerging wings of Sarpanch, the very move was watered down for political compulsions (Behar, 2003).

GS rose to eminence in Kerala for different reasons. The People's Campaign, which commenced on 17 August 1996, was the first attempt of planning from below with massive participation of rural people in real sense (Issac and Franke, 2000). Its main objective was to enable local bodies to prepare integrated plan projects in a scientific and participatory manner.[21] GS was involved in preparing village plan as per people's priority and mobilisation of local resources including labour. Such village plans were then integrated to district and state plan.

In the wake of people's campaign, attendance of people in the special GSs swelled to 27 lakh in August 1996, up from 8 lakh in April. The average participation for each GS was 180 people against total membership of 1,500. Women constituted about 25 per cent of total participants. Though the presence of 10 per cent rural electorate is not trivial, it is also noteworthy that such an extent of participation could be achieved only after widespread publicity, many seminars, use of ingenious methodology and involvement of over 1 lakh resource-persons. At the same time, there were significant inter-region, inter-district, inter-block and inter-GP variations (Issac and Franke, 2000). Most studies found that participation rate was high among SCs and poor and significantly lower among forward caste members and economically affluent sections. And the attendance rate plummeted in subsequent meetings (John and Chathukulam, 1999).

CPM dominated GPs recorded higher participation rates, in absolute figures and gender terms. This is not surprising as the campaign was designed and spearheaded by CPM and the party mobilised people directly and through its ancillary organisations. The opposition UDF partners were reluctant to support the campaign for political reasons and were also sceptical about budgetary allocation to GPs under their control. However, the participation in CPM controlled GPs did not see significant change in subsequent years, indicating that CPM could not build on the initial successes.[22] Moreover, political divisions raised ugly heads in GS meetings, opposition party supporters were discouraged, parallel meetings held and conflicts and disruptions marred the meetings.[23]

Gram Sabha in West Bengal

The panchayat system in West Bengal has had a rather shaky and languishing start. The exuberance evident in many other states after the recommendations of Mehta Committee, 1957 was virtually absent and the state initially displayed unconcerned outlook. The West Bengal Panchayat Act, 1957, the first attempt to rework the colonial network of local government, was perfunctory in nature and incompatible with the all-India pattern. The panchayat system lacked well-defined structures and democratic elements. However, it is noteworthy that when panchayat system really took off during 1978, it outmanoeuvred many other states on several counts, thus resembling with the proverbial race of the tortoise and hare. Many states might have started with a bang but the late and steady start of West Bengal outpaced others.

Broad reasons explaining the late start of panchayat system in West Bengal may be in order. Two factors—the outlook of the then political leadership and the electoral strategy pursued by the ruling party—would probably explicate the inertia and prevarication.

Till early 1960s Chief Minister B.C. Roy administered the state almost unilaterally. The agreed pattern was that B.C. Roy would run the government and P.C. Ghosh would look after the organisations of Congress party and each would not encroach upon other's sphere. Though B.C. Roy is regarded as the architect of modern Bengal, he was one urbanite per excellence with little understanding of agrarian problems. Neither was he very sympathetic to the Nehruvian ideal of community development or panchayat. His focus was on modernisation of infrastructure, setting up of industrial projects and communication network, through which rural development was supposed to come by. To one account (Ghosh et al., 2003: 174), his perception about rural local bodies hovered around providing the basic amenities to villagers for which the institution like Union Board would have been enough.

That the apathy of B.C. Roy was one explanatory factor becomes clear from the initiatives of P.C. Ghosh who did have roots in rural society and commitment to panchayat. Within a year after becoming Chief Minister, he initiated measures like passing the Panchayat Act, 1963, extension of panchayat coverage and constitution of four-tier panchayat in 1964. He also attempted delegation of fund and development programmes to panchayats and appointed one committee to suggest measures for strong decentralisation. However, he did not have much time and favourable ambience for translating his vision into reality. Since 1965, the political situation in West Bengal began to be more and more chaotic and violent.

After independence, the Bengal unit of Congress party did not have any specific political mobilisation strategy. For years, the organisational axiom was based on pampering the intermediaries—composed of landed gentry, moneylenders and leaders of village factions—on whom the rural poor had to depend heavily for livelihood. This intermediate class exploited its position, network and patron-client relationship and offered electoral support to Congress party—in most cases they themselves grabbed the public posts. As any serious threat from the opposition parties was not imminent and as the electoral win was more or less assured, the Congress leadership remained contented and did not contemplate alternate mobilisation strategy. However, the socio-political bases of the intermediate class also conditioned the perception of the leadership—direct contact with villagers could have undermined the dominant role of the class. That panchayat system could have embedded political footings among vast rural population, broadened the social bases of the leadership did not either dawn to the Congress leadership or it was impervious to such potentiality. When the Left Front government came to the state power with massive mandate in 1977, it realised the immense potential of panchayat and reaped political dividends for decades.

The Panchayat Act, 1957 abolished erstwhile Union Board and established two-tier panchayat units: Gram Panchayat at village and Anchal Panchayat at Union level. Later on, the West Bengal Zilla Parishad Act, 1963 introduced two higher tiers—Anchalik Parishad at block and Zilla Parishad at district level. The 1957 and 1963 acts together established four-tier panchayat system, a contrast to the three-tier in other states. Gram Panchayat and Anchal Panchayat came into existence during 1958–59 when phase by phase elections were held. Full fledged four-tier commenced from 2 October, 1964 for the entire state, except in few blocks of Bardhaman, Darjeeling and Jalpaiguri districts. However, the two higher tiers met their inglorious death as soon as they were born—all were superseded on 23 April, 1969 by one executive fiat.[24]

One noteworthy feature of the Panchayat Act, 1957 was that the democratic principle was envisaged only for the Gram Panchayat members. The state government was empowered to constitute Gram Sabha at every village comprising all persons registered in the electoral roll of the state assembly. This Gram Sabha—with about 1,300 voters on average—would directly elect from amongst themselves 9–15 members of Gram Panchayat. The Gram Panchayat members would have to elect one Adhayaksha (Chairperson) and Upa-Adhyaksha. The Gram Sabha was to meet at least twice a year and its foremost responsibilities extended to consideration of annual budget, administrative report, giving direction and advice to Gram Panchayat in the sphere of formulation of development plan, particularly agricultural production. The Gram Sabha meeting was to be convened by Adhyaksha or Upa-Adhyaksha by giving extensive circulation of meeting notice, informing the date, time and agenda through beating of drums by village Chowkidar [u/s 3 (3)].

Though it was intended to ensure people's participation in the affairs of the Gram Panchayat, the Gram Sabha under the 1957 Act did have illusory existence. Its meetings were not held regularly and as per the stipulations.[25] The quorum could scarcely be achieved. Poor information dissemination was strongly associated with low attendance of the members. The people did not have clear perception about the powers and role of the Gram Sabha. They could not differentiate between the Gram Sabha and Gram Panchayat. The public interest and involvement could not be aroused also because the powers of the Gram Sabha were elementary. The Gram Sabha could consider budget of the Gram Panchayat, its annual administrative reports but it did not have the power to approve, pass or modify those. The Gram Panchayat members preferred casual approach, they hardly bothered about the Gram Sabha and were guided more by the Anchal Panchayat and Block Extension Officer. The Gram Panchayat was least powerful or autonomous and it was incapacitated to undertake development works or consider proposals coming from the Gram Sabha meetings. The resource base of the Gram Panchayat was weak, it could not tap own resource and the grants from government were infrequent and meagre.

A Strong Start

Few initiatives during late 1960s to restructure the panchayat system proved abortive due to political instability. The then ruling Congress government enacted one comprehensive panchayat act in 1973, which remains still now the basic legislation, though many amendments and modifications have transformed its fundamental character.[26] It is interesting to note why the same government that was earlier lukewarm to panchayat, passed the 1973 enactment and why the government did not keep its declared promise of holding panchayat election during 1974. One insistence is that the 1973 panchayat act was an attempt to build and consolidate rural support base and to ward off steady inroads of the left parties. But the government did not have the capacity to implement such a progressive legislation. The Congress party was fatally faction-ridden and its organisational base was in shambles, as a result coercive power was frequently invoked to suppress discontent and dissent. The leadership did not have the time and energy to attempt rural reconstruction and the "atrocious" emergency era turned everything upside down.

The West Bengal Panchayat Act, 1973 has replaced the erstwhile four-tier by one uniform three-tier structure: Gram Panchayat (GP) for a cluster of villages, Panchayat Samity (PS) for each administrative block and Zilla Parishad (ZP) for every district. Ironically, this act initially dispensed with the institution of Gram Sabha set up by 1957 act.[27]

The Left Front Government (LFG) after making four amendments to the 1973 act, conducted panchayat elections in June, 1978. This election is the watershed in the annals of panchayati raj in India. This is the first time when open elections with direct participation of political parties were held for filling up thousands of posts in all panchayat tiers. LFG can justifiably claim credit for holding successive panchayat elections on a clockwork precision. The political commitment of LFG to panchayat system is not only commendable but also unparallel.

It needs emphasis that the election to and constitution of panchayats in West Bengal was made on that national backdrop when Panchayati Raj in general was virtually in moribund condition and when the report of Ashok Mehta Committee, 1978 was yet to be published. Moreover, the instance evinces that the regenerative effort could be undertaken and panchayat system could be sustained even without constitutional support and this also raises one incidental question about the motive that propelled the move of LFG.

The probable reasons accounting for the move of LFG lie in the distinct political ideology of the left parties and the pragmatic effort of LFG to consolidate political power. Ideologically, the left parties are committed to the cause and interest of the poor peasantry that demands one institutional mechanism for mobilisation and offering political power to the poor. Without the countervailing institutional power of the state, it is difficult to break the dominance of rural rich and secure the cooperation of lower level bureaucracy in implementing land reforms measures, goes one argument. Local government has intrinsic importance in furthering and consolidating political power. For CPM, Satyabrata Sen was the first leader who realised during early 1969, how politically important panchayats could be for spreading and entrenching the political hold in vast rural stretches and Promod Dasgupta extended active support to such conviction. After assuming state power, LFG endeavoured to spread its wings in rural Bengal, where its political hold was relatively weak at that time. Another consideration was that a solid rural support base would help averting any possible overthrowing attempt on the part of the central government. On electoral terms, the rural support is more decisive than the urban front, not only numerically but also of the fact that the vicissitudes of industrial conditions may weaken the urban support bases over a longer period of time. At the same time, the peasant rebellion during 1969–71 at the behest of Naxalites also compelled LFG to ponder over how to prevent recurrence of peasant uprising as well as to neutralise future threat from ultra-left parties. Here, land reform and panchayat system converged for ideological, political and administrative reasons. Somewhat shedding the conventional orthodoxy, LFG realistically moved towards solidification of political power through (liberal) democratic system. This necessitated the creation of local democratic institutions forming integral part of the overall governance that would afford representation of poor peasantry, undermine the collusion of landed elites and bureaucracy and improve the delivery of basic services. That such reform is perfectly within the constitutional scheme, thus steer clear of any backlash from the central government also reinforced the case for the regenerative effort.[28] In fact, panchayat system has all through been conditioned by and embedded in the state politics and all political parties perceive panchayat as the conduit for expanding and firming up political and electoral bases (Gupta, 2010: 193). And West Bengal is not any exception, though the extent to which panchayat can serve the political interests of the ruling party is exemplified by the West Bengal experiment, perhaps more expressively than elsewhere.

Gram Sansad and Gram Sabha: Functional Expanse

After the notional existence and inconsequential role performance of the Gram Sabha established by the panchayat act,

1957 rural people of West Bengal had to wait long for getting one popular assembly. The 1992 amendment (West Bengal Act of XVII of 1992) introduced one structure of Gram Sabha with the objective of mass participation and empowerment of panchayat. Because of higher density of population, one composite Gram Sabha was considered unwieldy as far as participation of people was concerned, thus Gram Sabha was for each and every GP ward. However, after the 73rd Amendment Act, one legal anomaly cropped up. As per the definition of the 73rd Amendment Act, GS is a body comprising all electorate within a village panchayat. In this sense there would be many Gram Sabhas in a single GP of West Bengal. To clear the legal contradiction[29] another amendment in 1994 (West Bengal Act of XVIII of 1994) renamed the earlier Gram Sabha as the Gram Sansad (hereafter *only* Sansad) and introduced one additional composite unit of the Gram Sabha (hereafter *only* Sabha) for the entire territorial area of a GP. Thus, from 1994 onwards, two distinct yet integrated tiers of GS are working in West Bengal. Moreover, 2003 amendment act has envisaged another set of participatory platforms—Block Sansad, Zilla Sansad and above all Gram Unnayan Samity, whose composition, functions and role performance have been detailed in Chapter 4.

Sansad is composed of all persons whose names are included in the electoral roll of West Bengal legislative assembly pertaining to the area of a GP ward, as demarcated on the basis of number of electorates. Every Sansad shall hold two meetings in a year: half yearly in November and annual in May. However, extraordinary meeting may be called at any time if the situation so demands or if the state government so directs (u/s 16A (2). The date, place and time of meeting are to be fixed by GP. It requires emphasis that if any GP does not follow the stipulation of two meetings every year, it will be bereft of grants of the state government and Finance Commission. The Pradhan (Chairperson of GP), or Upa-Pradhan or the elected GP member from the ward concerned will preside over Sansad meeting. Presence of 10 per cent of total members is the prescribed quorum, without which the meeting will stand adjourned and the next one will be held after 7 days at the same time, place and with same agenda. Ironically, there is no quorum for such adjourned meeting.

Sansad "shall" guide and advice GP with regard to the schemes for economic development and social justice within its area (u/s 16A). It "may" also identify or lay down principles for identification of the schemes required to be taken up on priority basis for economic development of the village; identify or lay down principle for identification of the beneficiaries for various poverty alleviation programmes; constitute Gram Unnayan Samity with such functional committees as may be required; mobilise mass participation of people for community welfare programmes or for adult education, family and child welfare; promote solidarity and harmony among all sections of people; and record its objection to any action of the Pradhan or GP member for failure to implement any development scheme properly or without active participation of the people of the area concerned.

Apart from the aforesaid general powers, every Sansad shall also take up few other agenda items for deliberation, recommendation and suggestion: in half-yearly meeting, GP budget for the following year and latest report on the audit and accounts of GP and in annual meeting supplementary budget for the previous year, GP report on works already done or proposed to be taken up in following year, amount received by GP from different sources and amount actually spent on different items of work and the list of beneficiaries (u/s 18).

Institutionally, Sansad has been entrusted with significant powers and functions which smack of civic participation, democratic as well as developmental dynamism. It will identify development schemes as per the perceived priority of the villagers, identify individual beneficiaries, scrutinise the role of GP members in the scheme implementation process. Its role regarding civic participation extends to mobilisation of people's participation for community welfare programme, social solidarity and integrity.

Gram Sabha, on the other hand, will have one meeting in a year, ordinarily in December, after completion of half-yearly

Sansad meetings. Its meeting will be presided over by the Pradhan or Upa-Pradhan. Presence of five per cent of total members will form quorum and no quorum will be required for adjourned meeting, if any. The powers and functions of Sabha are almost identical to Sansad (u/s 16B (7), only addition being its aggregating role. GP "shall" collect and coordinate the resolutions of Sansads and place those together with its view and action taken report to Sabha for deliberation and recommendation. All questions coming before Sabha and points raised therein shall be referred to GP for its consideration. It is to be noted that few important functions like consideration or approval of annual plan, annual budget of GP are not integral part of Sabha meetings.

Few commonalities are evident for Sansad and Sabha meetings. For every meeting a seven-day notice is required. The proceedings of the meeting will have to be recorded, read out before conclusion of meeting. Though decision by majority vote is the prescribed rule for GP, no reference as to how decision will be taken in meeting is conspicuous. However, decision by consensus, not by majoritarian principle, is informally expected.

The panchayat act categorically confers binding status to Sansad resolutions. Every Sansad resolution "shall" be duly considered by GP in its meeting. GP decision and action in this regard shall form part of the report concerning works done or proposed to be done that will have to be placed before Sansad, Sabha meetings and before Panchayat Samiti (PS) and other prescribed authority.

If GP fails to act on Sansad resolution or does not place supplementary budget, budget for coming year, audit report, report on works, amount received and utilised or list of beneficiaries, that will have serious adverse consequences. When considered in the overall perspective, such omission will be an act of impropriety and irregularity (u/s 17A) that will come under the purview of Auditor's report or will be deemed as wilful omission or refusal to carry out the provisions of the Panchayat Act that may lead to the removal of the Pradhan/Upa-Pradhan (u/s 213(1), or will be an incompetence to perform or default in performance of the duties that may ultimately lead to supersession of GP (u/s 214). In other words, any negligence or failure on the part of GP to hold Sansad meeting, circulation of meeting notice, recording of public attendance and proceedings and to carry out assigned functions will invite penal clauses enshrined in the panchayat act itself.

However, the legal status of Sabha resolutions is not much exalting. The eminence of Sansad is gradually increasing and that of Sabha is waning. The resolution adopted at Sabha meetings shall be considered by GP and its decision and action on those will form a part of the report on works that has to be placed before Sansad and Sabha meetings for discussion and recommendation.[30] One substantial power of Sabha relates to the discussion and recommendation relating to the resolutions of Sansad within the GP area. However, one anomalous situation may creep in. Both Sansad and Sabha can deliberate, recommend and suggest on matters which are almost similar. If one unit of Sansad adopts a resolution contradicting the other, which one will prevail? While GP shall consider Sansad resolution, what will happen if Sabha takes resolution contravening that of Sansad(s)? The general impression is that Sansad has the overriding importance. But each Sansad is concerned with local issues and priorities which are divergent across wards (if different parties hold ward seats, the situation will be trickier). The resolution of each Sansad must be compiled and coordinated into one plan of action. If GP does it that would effectively eat into the importance of the public forum. One viable option may be to confer final coordinating power to Sabha over Sansad resolutions.

Block and Zilla Sansad

The concept of Sansad has subsequently been extended to other panchayat tiers. West Bengal Panchayat Amendment Act, 2003 has introduced two novel structures—Block Sansad and Zilla Sansad. Every PS shall have one Block Sansad that will consist of all GP and PS members pertaining to the block. It will have two meetings every year (u/s 115A). Every ZP, similarly, will have Zilla Sansad comprising all GP Pradhan, PS

Sabhapati, Sahakari-Sabhapati and Karmadhyakhaya and all ZP members and it will have two meetings per year.

Both Block and Zilla Sansad shall guide and advise respective tier on matters relating to development including preparation of annual plan, budget, implementation of development programmes, schemes for economic development and social justice. Any member of such Sansad is entitled to demand in writing to the Executive Officer of the tier concerned for placement of any document like audit report, budget, annual action plan in the meeting. The deliberation, recommendation and observation of each Sansad shall be considered by the tier concerned within one month of such meeting and its decision and action taken report shall be placed in the next meeting.

Block and Zilla Sansads have strengthened the organic linkage among panchayat tiers. Even a GP Pradhan will now be able to seek information and place development demands to the action plan of ZP, for instance. The transparency in the panchayat system gets vindicated when its activity reports are to be placed in open meeting and before the elected members of lower tiers even.

What transpires is that far more expansive and comprehensive participatory space has been made open for the rural people in West Bengal. If Kerala involved GS more extensively in development planning and social mobilisation and Gram Swaraj in Madhya Pradesh entrusted sweeping decision-making powers directly to GS, West Bengal institutionalises participatory planks covering perhaps all points of the compass. Notwithstanding such spatial design, the crucial question is whether the newly introduced institutions are evoking interest and catering to the wishes of villagers or whether these institutions are emerging as the fountainhead of local development and democracy. However, one rider is in order. Designing institution, endowing powers is one thing and making those functional and real is quite another. The Indian irony is that (too) many legal frames are there but most of these flounder on hard rock of reality.

Performance Appraisal in West Bengal

Regarding the process and outcome of GS, West Bengal is one absorbing, if not intriguing case, where contradictory claims confuse the canvas. Unlike most other states where the performance of GS is almost unvaryingly unsatisfactory, the situation in West Bengal is not that straightforward. Some writers, taking a positive stand insist that the working and performance of the village assemblies is relatively better and it is on the ascending graph. Few other assessment reports, on the contrary, reveal a pattern not fundamentally different from other states.

The claim is that Sansad in particular is one important institutional innovation that has contributed to the ideals of participatory governance. Villagers know about the existence of Sansad. Its meetings are held, the average attendance rate is not negligible and people of all age groups participate (Datta and Bhattacharyya, 2000). Even in those districts that have lower literacy rates, the attendance rates are noteworthy. The deliberation in Sansad is somewhat structured—agenda setting, monitoring, review and designing projects (Ghatak et al., 2002). A lot of heat is generated in Sansad meetings—formation of Beneficiary Committee had always been a subject of debate and discussion, people even walked out when the Pradhan refused to concede their demands (Datta and Bhattacharyya, 2000). The beneficiaries are consulted about the schemes to be taken up and the project sites to be selected. The meetings centre on practical and concrete problems of the village and participants accept collective decisions even when these do not coincide with their individual choice.[31] One report contended that the attendant rates—even when declining—compare fairly well with other countries where there is emphasis on people's participation and the villagers feel that their involvement and participation in GS meetings and panchayat activities is worthwhile (HDR, 2004: 68). When about 75 per cent participants belong to *bargadars* and *pattadars*, the poor sections are "evidently gaining not only from land reforms but also from the process of decentralisation". The overall performance record is encouraging especially when compared to other states where panchayat elections are not held regularly and GS meetings are not often convened.

The participants in Sansad meetings demand new programmes like installation of tube-well, supply of seed, fertiliser, drinking water, draining out saline water and more work opportunity (for women). They select location of projects like road, plan physical details of repair of road. More common and widespread is the monitoring and review functions where villagers raise question about failure of a project, poor quality of work, non-release of fund for sanctioned project and neglect of the felt needs. Landless labourers ask why the wage employment programmes are taken up only during monsoon when they can otherwise get work opportunities. Women members resent diversion of fund, say, from nutritional programme for women. Insufficient and injudicious utilisation of fund also generates debate (Ghatak et al., 2002). Tersely, the works done and the role of GP members and local officials come under public scrutiny and somewhere mistakes had reportedly been admitted. The Sansad meetings are not mere endorsement of what party leaders propose and participants are not pointedly passive.

Even when some villagers are convinced that if they do not attend Gram Sabha meetings (during pre-1994 era) and act unitedly "the government will be out of power" and "the Jotedar will not give us (them) work" (Lieten, 2003: 224), all of them need not attend and speak in the meetings. Party leaders maintain constant contact and visit households where the people communicate their needs. Few 'poor villagers' who speak in meetings actually voice the collective demands of the locality. Moreover, "the leaders are abreast of the situation and as long as they take just decision, there is no need to butt in with remarks which may be off the mark" (Lieten, 1996: 197). Both Webster (1992) and Lieten (1996; 2003) maintained that there are many other informal or non-statutory fora where villagers express their views, which come back to GP for discussion and policy decision.

One outcome is that people get *gyan* (knowledge) from such public meetings and this is transmitted back to the household members (Lieten, 1996: 197). Such *gyan* pertains, inter alia, to the very importance of such meetings, practice of hygiene, regular schooling and information about procedural aspects of public loan programmes, leasing out pump set for minor irrigation and latest wage rates.

Few micro studies, on the other hand, divulge the lack of people's enthusiasm, high degree of politicisation and strong party control over local democratic institutions which obfuscate the spontaneous participation of people and undermine the prospect of village assembly. Because of interplay of several factors Sansad stumbles to emerge as the platform of villagers and the barriers holding up the fructification of local democracy are yet to be overcome.

The working of Sansad seems to be "highly disappointing". GP members show scant interest, little publicity is given to such meetings, lack of quorum is widespread and only formality is observed. The same villagers who turn out massively for voting and party related activities like campaign and fund raising, show aversion when it comes to Sansad meetings. The people express doubt about the utility of Sansad as a forum for venting their grievances against under-performance of GP and they do not utilise Sansad effectively.[32]

Sansad meetings are more a ritual than a participatory process (Thorlind, 2001). One graphic description is indicative. The meeting started at 7 PM with one lamp at the table and the rest in dark. Only 130 (of total 1,000) members came to the meeting mainly because of call of the Pradhan. Those people were beneficiaries of some programmes (Jain, 2002: 19). The Pradhan appraised the activities undertaken by GP, informed about proposed schemes and placed GP accounts, all in one go. He harped on the fact that many development works had to be postponed because of lack of fund. Three members raised questions about non-completion of road repair programme, poor functioning of Anganwadi centre and non-availability of teachers in local school. The meeting lasted for 90 minutes. However, most participants did not have a fair idea about the significance and role of Sansad.

The government figures relating to the holding of meetings and extent of people's participation disclose few trends rather unequivocally (Table 2.2 and Appendix 2). In no year all the Sansad and Sabha meetings have ever been held everywhere, in some years the proportion of adjourned and cancelled meetings had been astonishingly high and worrisome. The average attendance rate hovered around 11 per cent for Sansad and 5 per cent for Sabha meetings—that is just around the benchmark. However, the average figures conceal more than disclosing the pattern: in some districts the rate is well below the quorum and in some districts it is as high as 70 per cent. The attendance rates almost evenly dip in the half yearly Sansad meetings, authenticating that people are more inclined to selection of beneficiaries than the planning functions (as per the stipulation for yearly meeting). For Sabha meetings just bare minimum attendance implies gradual erosion of its importance and utility in the eyes of villagers.[33]

Table 2.2

Attendance of People in Gram Sansad Meetings in West Bengal

Year	*No. of Sansad*	*May*		*November*	
		Meetings held (%)*	*Average Attendance (%)*	*Meetings held* (%)*	*Average Attendance (%)*
1996	36125	NA	NA	89	18
1997	36179	29	15	88	18
1998	44506	97	NA	99	16
1999	44634	95	12	98	13
2000	45167	97	12	96	13
2001	45167	97	12	95	11
2002	45094	97	12	72	11
2006	45168	90	11	97	8.5

* Include those reconvened meetings held after adjournment for lack of quorum.

Source: Annual Report 2003–2007. Department of Panchayat and Rural Development, Government of West Bengal, and *Panchayati Raj Samachar.*

Sansad is overwhelmingly a male forum (Ghatak et al., 2002: 50). Participation of women and other minority and vulnerable groups is uniformly low. A section of poor does not evince interest as they remain busy with subsistence struggle. People belonging to SC, ST keep away as they perceive their inability in the party structure which is dominated by higher caste leadership (Ghatak et al., 2002: 51). Relatively affluent also shy away as no possible benefits can come in their way. Such negative wealth bias is related to the fact that those meetings deal primarily with welfare programmes for the poor.

Those who attend happen to be the members or supporters of the ruling party at the helm of GP. The supporters of the party that does not hold panchayat power or those people not directly associated with party politics stay away from meetings because they feel their opinion will have little impact on the outcome of such meetings. Indeed, majority commentators concur that the ruling party supporters predominantly throng the meetings and the opposition camp stay away (Ghatak et al., 2002; Jain, 2002; Kumar, 2006, Sen and Yasin, 2007). And this feature is common both in left and right party dominated GPs. For instance, in one Congress party ruled GP, only 33 people (out of 1,200) bothered to attend and all but one was the ruling party supporter (Majumdar, 2009: 87).

While the extent of people's participation in GS meetings has been found comparatively lower in West Bengal (Kumar, 2006: 206), the participants tend to remain mute spectators. Seen overall, the motive of participation seems to show solidarity or gratitude and for the prospective beneficiaries it is to remain in the good books of the local leaders. Thus, the meetings are basically for the ruling party 'sympathisers' and 'favour seekers' (Ghatak et al., 2002; Jain, 2002, Corbridge et al., 2003; Bhattacharya, M., 2002; Bhattacharyya, H., 2002).

Only a handful people generally speak in such meeting. Even those having had active participatory records do no speak (Corbridge et al., 2003). People do not complain when they have the opportunity, when they do not receive benefits and when they find the quality of public service unsatisfactory (Kumar, 2006: 227). While there is a set pattern not to allow general villagers to make critical assessment of GP activities, thus defeating the very objective of participation,[34] those who would actually speak are handpicked beforehand by the leaders of ruling party. At the informal *Gram Baithak* (meeting) with people affiliated to the party, it is decided which persons would propose what scheme in Sansad. Such Baithak serves the role in stage management and rehearsal of participation to be acted in the statutory forum. This sort of strategy indicates formally that it is not the party leaders but villagers who are proposing the schemes/beneficiaries and it apparently testifies the power of the people, while everything is tokenism. The actual decisions are taken by party leaders outside of Sansad for the disclosed reason that decision-making at public meetings involves conflict and tension. People's participation in Sansad is not anyway to criticise or challenge the power structure—it is all about routinisation of power (Corbridge et al., 2003: 2382).[35]

A strong association has been found between higher land-holdings and public speaking in Sansad meetings, though not in participation. Among those participants who spoke and intervened in discussions, the proportion of landless and marginal landholders was substantially lower than the higher landholding classes (Bardhan et al., 2009: 52). Big farmers, because of their superior educational status, could use the public forum more often and effectively. Such contentions corroborate what Webster (1992: 99) observed earlier: "one can clearly understand the difficulty of an illiterate labourer in even believing that he has something to say let alone to try and express his thought in the same forum and on the same basis as a local teacher or high caste Brahmin member of the CPM".

Because of unsatisfactory working and outcome of GS, some states have already urged people not to take GS meetings casually and they have also arranged video-taping of the meeting. The situation might not have reached such a pass in West Bengal. Yet, the Department of Panchayat and Rural Development publishes advertisements and uses graffiti requesting people to attend the meetings. The Department once kept close vigil and sent observers for documenting and reporting back to the Department. The overall picture gleaned from such reports is more or less saddening (Roy, 2001). Many

Pradhans and Upa-Pradhans displayed repugnancy. The average people's attendance rate lingered around 13–14 per cent. In many instances, the activity and accounts reports were formally read out without having or allowing discussion and debate. The discussion revolved around beneficiary committee, centrally sponsored schemes and maternity allowance, etc. There was clear lack of effective two-way communication, feedback and lack of endeavour on the part of GP members to involve people. There was no evidence of meeting of minds, creative or constructive consensus (Roy, 2001: 438–39). Not surprisingly therefore, the poor villagers felt alienated and exhibited inertia.

The process of consultation on development works has been found restricted to the close circle of GP members and local party leaders. The availability and control over development funds offered GP members the scope and they played a role almost similar to the traditional headman (William, 1999: 235). The development works were personalised and panchayat funds were used to building political support base. The welfare funds went certainly to the economically deserving groups, but only to those politically well connected. Such partisan role was not absent earlier, but it had now become the norm (William, 1999: 236).

When people in general, disassociate themselves from Sansad and Sabha meetings and when such a trend is decried by party documents,[36] the political parties, of all hues, desist from taking steps towards encouraging and entrenching people's participation (Sen and Yasin, 2007: 195). The party leaders tend to feel complacent and remain obsessed with building a myth about the organisational and managerial capacity of the party. They make gullible villagers to believe that the party has provided the best model of governance and whatever it could not deliver is due to the legal constraints. They also propagate the notion that panchayats are for distributing state largesse and not the institution of village governance (Kumar, 2006: 232). The political leaders consciously pursue a strategy to hold back information on development schemes, refrain from playing wider conscientisation role or arousing people's expectation beyond the capacity of panchayats (Corbridge et al., 203: 2382).

Summing up

After enervating legal endowment and not much proficuous performance during pre-amendment period, GS has been resuscitated with statutory recognition and endowment of powers and functions. This reincarnation has the potential to culminate in one robust, dynamic, unique and innovative institution and process at the grassroots. However, it transpires that GS still remains as languishing and lofty as ever in most states including West Bengal. Majority GS meetings are convened 'only with some inducement of powers, offer of grants, whip of a party or fiat of government'. People's participation is not impulsive, open, constructive and development centred discussion is not evident everywhere. Most participants are prospective beneficiaries of the public programmes and they are more intent on securing the approval of their candidature for benefits rather than community concerns. GP members are not always amenable to the idea of popular review of their decisions and they are wary of possible usurpation of their decision-making prerogative.

Few broad and general trends manifest from the working experience of GS across states.

- Villagers do not always get the information about GS meeting well in advance. The agenda items are straight-jacketed and inflexible.
- Meetings are convened not usually as per statutory prescription. Yet, the prevailing penal provisions are rarely invoked.
- Quorum is hardly achieved in majority of the meetings. Diverse strategies are deliberately used to fulfil the legal requirement.
- Participation of people and their interest in GS meetings is gradually waning. Many villagers might have initially attended out of curiosity and with high hopes but when they found that the meeting has not much to decide and

the deliberation has not much practical outcome, their interest frittered away.

- The dilemma is: if few people come, the credibility of GS suffers and if many people attend, the meeting can lead to chaos and cleavages.
- GS meetings are getting formalised and standardised: podium, sitting arrangement, refreshment, introduction of guests, reading out few reports and long lecture. They are becoming more like public (party) meetings where GP President, officials (and others) deliver lectures and people listen and get *gyan*. Interaction and constructive debate is neither preferred nor practised. At best, some scheme specific information is passed on to the villagers.
- There is little constructive discussion and concrete decision. The meetings are more about talking, discussion and less about taking decision or seeking solution to development problems.
- The resolutions adopted in meetings are rarely read out, people seldom get to know what decisions have finally been approved.
- Not much follow-up action is evident or reported in the next meeting.
- The attendance of people and the quality of deliberation improve perceptibly when civil society organisations take initiatives to make villagers aware and mobilise them for GS meetings. In such cases GP President can be forced to do a lot of explaining and has to take public suggestion seriously. However, such intervention and consequent positive outcome is sporadic and isolated.

The general indifference of people and the unsatisfactory performance of GS raise few fundamental questions: why the statutory endowment does not make much impact on enhancing the interest of the cross-sections of villagers, why the participants remain passive, why they do not challenge non-transparency, misappropriation of funds or incidence of corruption and why people do not enforce accountability.

During the pre-amendment period the apathy of the people was believed to be because of powerlessness of GS

(GoI, 1963: 12).[37] Neither GS was empowered nor was there any attempt at GS to redress or solve the basic needs and problems of villagers. A huge gap between the public demands and the capacity of GP persisted. In the face of prevarication of their demands, the people perceived GS as insensitive, cloutless and dispensable body. The incapacity of GS put GP members in a predicament and stunted their enthusiasm. In short, the approach to GS was piecemeal and its powers were parochial.

People are unlikely to come—by forfeiting a day's wage or skipping important engagement—unless the opportunity cost of participation is commensurate with the possible benefits. If GS does not have the power to satisfy at least a part of the demands/requirements of villagers, people cannot be enthused. It is futile to expect that people will flock together to hear what GP will do in future, what it did previously or what it could not do because of paucity of fund, etc.

If the powerlessness of GS was the most important reason for the indifference of people and frivolity of GS, the situation ought to have improved after statutory endowment. One may, of course, argue that GS still does not deal with issues like education, agriculture, nutrition or livestock that have significant bearing on people's lives. Surely, the powers of GS are inadequate and basically aspirational in nature. But what it has already got is not trivial or inconsequential either. Now, GS can set the agenda in development process, review the GP activities and select beneficiaries.

At least in Kerala, Madhya Pradesh and West Bengal, GS has been entrusted with formidable powers, it has autonomy of action and its decisions are almost binding on GP. Ironically, in those exalted cases even, the people's interest and involvement has not demonstratively constellated, only visible improvement is in the frequency and regularity of meetings. The overall trends seem to suggest that the conferment of important or overriding powers is not singularly significant and the accounting reasons are diverse and deep down.

Notes and References

1. Dreze, J. and Sen, A., 2002. *India: Development and Participation*. New Delhi: Oxford University Press.
2. The Mehta Committee, 1978 recommended only for a village level committee to be composed of elected Mandal and Zilla Parishad members and one representative of small and marginal farmers (p. 49). This committee, in its two meetings in every year, would explain to people the programmes the Mandal Panchayat was implementing in the area and would channel people's feedback to Mandal Panchayat (p. 81).
3. The PESA is applicable to 9 states namely, Andhra Pradesh, Chhattisgarh, Gujarat, Himachal Pradesh, Madhya Pradesh, Maharashtra, Jharkhand, Orissa and Rajasthan.
4. States are ignoring and violating the spirit and provisions of PESA. The Orissa Panchayat Act, for instance, provides that the customary mode of dispute resolution should be consistent with the relevant laws in force, in harmony with the tenets of the constitution and human rights. Madhya Pradesh has taken no step to amend its Forest Act, 1927 so as to seek GS permission before utilising natural resources. For detail scenario see Sharma, B.D. Committee Report, 2007. Ministry of Panchayati Raj, Government of India; Singh, S.K. ed., 2005. *Self Governance for Tribal*, Hyderabad: National Institute of Rural Development (Vol. I and II); Prabhu, Pradip, 2004. 'PESA and Illusions of Tribal Self Governance'. *Combat Law*, 2 (5).
5. Such as GoI, 1963; 2nd Administrative Reforms Commission, 2007. The (Draft) Model Panchayat and Gram Swaraj Act 2009 proposes Ward Sabha as one specific statutory tier below Gram Sabha.
6. Tamil Nadu does not have ward level unit. But it follows a practice where GS meetings are held in GP wards by rotation. But this practice cannot substitute the role and usefulness of ward level assembly.
7. Still then, members are not always serious. In one instance, Kerala State Election Commission found 400 GP members guilty of non-convening meetings (John, 2007: 236). And they were not possibly disqualified from GP membership.

8. Similar observations can be found in Sahai, Raghubir, 1968. *Panchayati Raj in India*. Allahabad: Kitab Mahal; Mathur, Narayan and Singh, 1966. *Panchayati Raj in Rajasthan: A Study in Jaipur District*. Delhi: Implex India.
9. Patil and Kittur,1990. 'Grassroots Democracy: Analysis of Gram Sabha'. *Political Science Review*, January-December, 72–83.
10. Raphael, Jose, 1990. *Decentralised Planning in Karnataka*. Poona (Pune): Centre for Development Studies and Activities (Mimeo.).
11. Aziz, Abdul, (1994: 124). *Decentralisation: Mandal Panchayat System in Karnataka* (1987–1992). Hyderabad: National Institute of Rural Development.
12. Meenakshisundaram, S,S., 1999. 'Gram Sabha: Lessons from Karnataka'. *Kurukshetra*, October.
13. Reddy and Bandi (2007: 255). 'Participatory Democracy: Role of Gram Sabha in Decentralised Governance', in Ram Sundar, ed. Few other instances are illustrative. Only 4000 (of total 9185) meetings scheduled on 2 October, 2001 were actually held in Rajasthan (source: *5th Estate*, November, 2001). In Chittraghatti GP of Bihar not a single meeting was held for last 5 years.
14. Behar, 2003; Despande et al., 2002; Ghatak et al., 2002; also Mathew, Gorge and Mathew, Ananda, 2005. 'India: Decentralisation and Local Governance—How Clietelism and Accountability Work', in Hadenius, Axel, ed., *Decentralisation and Democratic Governance Experiences from India, Bolivia and South Africa*. Stockholm: Almqvist & Wiksell International.
15. Narayana, D., 2005. *Institutional Change and Its Impact on the Poor and Excluded: The Indian Decentralisation Experience*. Working Paper No. 242. Organisation for Economic Co-operation and Development (OECD) and International Labour Organization.
16. Sivana, M. (2007: 129). 'Political Decentralisation and Issue of Accountability: The Case of Gram Sabha in Karnataka', in Ram Sundar, ed.
17. Das, M.K., 2000. 'Kerala's Decentralised Planning: Floundering Experiment'. *Economic & Political Weekly*, 2 December. Also Palanithurai et al., 2006.

18. Mathew, George and Mathew, Ananda, 2005, op. cit. See also Behar, 2003; Palanithurai et al., 2006.
19. One survey during October, 2003 by Charkha found that attendance was 5–15 per cent in 17 panchayats, 15–25 per cent in 23 and 25–40 per cent in 6 panchayats. Women attendance was nil in 12 panchayat, 5–10 per cent in 22 and 25 per cent in 21 panchayats. 35 per cent people participated in plan formulation and 28 per cent in plan implementation process (cited in *Panchayati Raj Update*. December, 2003, p. 6).
20. A Forest Committee was formed after 20 minutes discussion between the Sarpanch and department official (Johnson et al., 2005: 944).
21. One insistence was that the campaign is an attempt to get rid of political stalemate and economic stagnation [Jose, George, (1997: 89). 'Panchayat and Participatory Planning in Kerala', *Indian Journal of Public Administration*, 43, 1].
22. Chaudhuri, Shubham and Heller, Patrick, 2003. *The Plasticity of Participation: Evidence from a Participatory Governance Experiment*, Working Paper 03–01. Columbia University, Institute for Social and Economic Research and Policy.
23. The campaign later came under scanner. CAG Report, 2005 identified few fallacies of the big bang approach. The Campaign's emphasis was less on sustainable institutional capacity and more on meetings, conventions, involvement of political activists and training the resource persons at state expense whose durable benefits are unclear. Without building institutional capacity, development funds were provided generously without adequate safeguard. The campaign diluted the role of panchayat members and assigned key role to party activists and State Planning Board.
24. One explanation is that when Calcutta High Court annulled the election of Anchalik Parishad and Zilla Parishad, the state government, instead of reconstituting those, removed all members and appointed administrators (Banerjee, 2002: 66). Another contention is that the United Front government dissolved those as they were controlled by the Congress party members (Ghosh and Kumar, 2003: 176).

25. For instance, not a single meeting of Gram Sabha was held in 11 Blocks during 1966–67 (Mukhopadhyaya, Asoke, K. (1980: 58). *The Panchayat Administration in West Bengal*, Calcutta (Kolkata): The World Press).
26. For improving the functioning and furthering responsive local government, the 1973 act has been amended 25 times (up to March 2007).
27. However, during the intervening period one aborted Bill—West Bengal Panchayat Bill, 1969 (as amended by the Select Committee of West Bengal legislative assembly)—contained the provisions for Gram Sabha. Though the Bill renamed Gram Sabha as Gram Parishad, the composition, power, etc. was almost identical to 1957 act.
28. Though the normative and legal basis was prevalent at the national level, a set of circumstances and realistic thinking led to the panchayats being accepted as the 'optimal strategy' to promote the political goals of the ruling party and at the same time empower the poor in an effective way [Mitra, S.K., (2001: 113). 'Making Local Government Work: Local Elites and Governance', in Kohli, ed.]
29. Ghosh, B. (2000: 315). 'West Bengal', in Mathew, G, ed., *Status of Panchayati Raj In India and Union Territories*. New Delhi: Concept.
30. Under section 16(7) of West Bengal Panchayat Act, the Gram Sabha cannot question the constitution of Beneficiary Committee to be formed by Gram Sansad. When the 2003 amendment entirely substituted Beneficiary Committee by Gram Unnayan Samity, one does not know why such a provision still persists. It might imply final authority of Sansad over constitution of a committee. But when one executive order of 10 December, 2008 takes away Sansad's power to form Gram Unnayan Samity, this provision becomes superfluous.
31. Datta, Prabhat (2003: 78). 'Participatory Rural Governance: the West Bengal Experience', *West Bengal Political Science Review*, VI (I and II), 69–82.
32. Kumar, Girish and Ghosh, B., (1996: 91). *West Bengal Panchayat Elections, 1993*. New Delhi: Concept.

33. During 2007, total 72 per cent (2342 out of 3242) Sabha meetings had been held. In Dakshin 24 Paragans no meeting could be held, in Murshidabad only 11 per cent was convened (*Panchayati Raj Samachar*, August–September, 2008, (p. 1).
34. Ghosh, D.K. (1999: 146). 'People's Participation in West Bengal Panchayat: Scope and Reality'. *Quarterly Journal of All India Institute of Local Self Government*, 70 (3).
35. Sansad is caught in the vortex of claims and counter-claims. Political leaders allege that people are less interested and they do not want to shoulder responsibilities. And people aver that by participating they can help neither themselves nor villagers. The political leaders do not give people the responsibility or take suggestions seriously (Bhattacharya, 2002: 133).
36. CPM concedes that GP leadership is not always serious about Sansad or receptive to people's suggestions. The party documents urge GP leadership to accept popular demands and explain to people why a particular demand cannot be fulfilled (Bhattacharya, M., 2002: 133; Bhattacharyya, H. 2002).
37. Diwankar Committee (GoI, 1963: 12–13) noted a sense of frustration stemming from the lack of effective powers to redress the grievances arising from bureaucratic functioning of the administration and of resources which led people away from GS.

3

People and Popular Assembly

> Today, the Panchayat system has to take three main directions: deepening the roots of democratic decentralization, strengthening self-governance of the Panchayats and institutionalising good governance in all the tiers of the system. Deepening the roots of democratic decentralization entails ensuring increasing participatory democracy at the level of the Gram Sangsad so that people who face social and economic discrimination irrespective of their political affiliations can play a central role in planning, implementing and monitoring development programmes at the village level. Empowerment of the people comes with the precondition that the right to information and the right to express their opinion on the functioning of the Panchayats is secure.[1]

Whether one accepts the above observation of the former panchayat minister of West Bengal as yet another avouchment or as one underhand admission of aberration from the earlier pledges, the fact remains that Panchayat Act of West Bengal has charted out quite comprehensive and powerful structures for popular participation. Their existence for about two decades implies that these structures have crossed the staggering stage of infancy and therefore they are in a position to broadly indicate the prospect, institutions like Sansad hold for deepening democracy.

As regards the subsequent delineation and exploration of people's involvement and their role in the deliberation and decision-making process of Sansad and Sabha, few limitations merit mention. The basic research tool for eliciting responses from the respondents was the formal interview with pre-tested questionnaire. Though unstructured discussion with villagers and GP functionaries was held at informal level, it has to be conceded that the interview is not one authoritative tool for grasping the dynamics of panchayat politics and its decision-making process: many internal factors, informal underpinnings are bound to miss attention. Why villagers attend or abstain from such meeting, how panchayat decisions are taken, what is the nature of party politics are few aspects that cannot be comprehended by formal interview only.

Surely, the legislative measures have brought local government apparatus down to the ward level; planning and implementation responsibilities have been assigned to them and people are supposed to be actively involved. However, the legal ordination does not work in a socio-political vacuum. Indeed, the rural politics and functional process of panchayats are inextricably linked to many informal practices and manoeuvrability (Ruud, 2003; Banerjee et al., 2005). For instance, despite the existence of powerful Sansad, people may not need to go and use Sansad forum because other extra-legal channels are available which may be advantageous and rewarding. Instead of the interview based investigation, one ethnographic study could have uncovered the roots of the panchayat process.

In some villages NGOs have initiated sensitisation programme, have made villagers aware, equipped and united for raising their voices and directing governance from below. In West Bengal the effort of one NGO in Nadia district had reportedly led to improved participation of people including women who demanded in Sansad meeting, scheme-information and virtually compelled the Pradhan to concede their demands.

It could have been absorbing to explore how the external intervention influences the nature of people's participation in the deliberation of Sansad and Sabha meetings. But in the sample GPs there was no NGO or similar organisations that ever operated or took up the cudgel. As such it has not been possible to peek at the probable impacts of community based organisation on the village fora.

As the analysis is based on the findings from only 10 GPs, any definite conclusions should be desisted. These can broadly be indicative patterns and any extrapolation for the state or other states should be done cautiously.

The survey was undertaken at that particular historical juncture when the very nature of panchayat politics in West Bengal was on a paradigmatic shift. For long 28 years the rural Bengal had witnessed almost unilateral sway of the Left parties (read CPM). The opposition parties (and junior partners of LFG) could enjoy influence in few pockets only. The panchayat script, dialogue, acting and direction all were under the tight strap of CPM. Only from mid-2006 such hegemony began to wane when Congress and Trinamul Congress gained footholds in many villages and posed strong challenge for the first time ever. Consequently, rural Bengal had seen many protest movements and political violence, leading to abrupt changes in the political perception and party allegiances of people, which might have influenced the responses of many villagers. And, for such an extraordinary situation, the survey results may be incongruous to the findings of many other studies in West Bengal.

Awareness

The process of democratisation is linked to people's knowledge and awareness about the structure, functions and their rights and responsibilities arising out of the public institution. Though awareness is usually related to the knowledge that arouses the awakening and spurs active involvement of people, thereby increasing the effectiveness of the institution, basic knowledge about the institution is not entirely insignificant. Employing awareness in a restrictive sense, the objective was to seek respondents' knowledge and acquaintance about the existence of Sansad, Sabha and the envisaged time slots of the assembly meetings. Moreover, the details of the functions, powers of those legal entities and villagers' rights therein were not sought.

The strong impression one gets from the responses of respondents is that they were fairly aware about the existence of Sansad, Gram Unnayan Samity (GUS) and they could specify the legally stipulated months of Sansad meetings (Figure 3.1). They were also able to identify the designation of speakers in Sansad meetings. In these respects, there was no significant variation across sample GPs. They had also heard the announcement of Sansad meeting (71%). It is only about GUS that lesser number of villagers was aware about it (59%) and this is understandable because this is one recently introduced structure, 10 years younger than Sansad and it was yet to be formed or to start functioning in many places.

Figure 3.1

Awareness of the Respondents

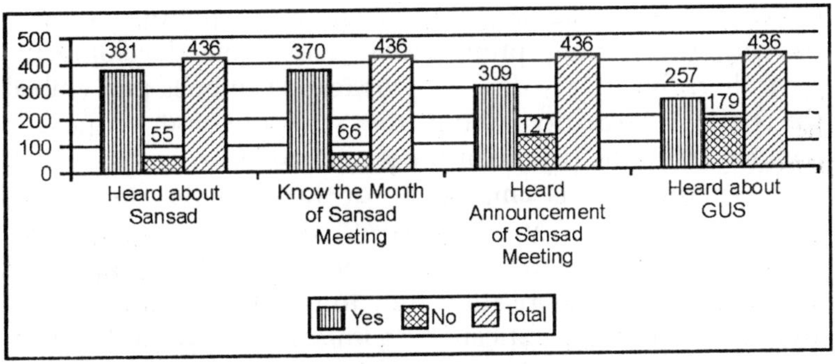

In many states the awareness of villagers about GS is low or lacking. For instance, in Kerala, a state with higher literacy rates and a state having undertaken massive people's campaign to involve the masses, the awareness level of villagers was found low, which is said to have perpetuated "low quality leadership and decision-making. Even though many of the elected representatives did not bother to convene Gram Sabha meetings, there was no popular upsurge against this vital breach of responsibility" (John, 2007: 236).

In the otherwise dejecting level of awareness elsewhere, the relatively higher level—even when assessed abstractly—in the survey responses may have been associated with the radical nature of peasant movements, agrarian reforms, high voltage political propaganda and the indispensability of panchayats in the lives of the villagers.

Since their institutionalisation with party based elections, panchayats have become the pivot around which agrarian reforms, development programmes and political mobilisation tend to be revolving. Indeed rural decentralisation has become the centre-pillar of the political campaigning of CPM. Party meetings are being recurrently held where the breakthroughs impacted and rural regeneration hastened by PRIs is mouthed routinely. In those meetings one would come across the claims about fundamental changes from the oppression of *Jotedars* to the reign of the poor people. To counter the propaganda onslaught of CPM, the opposition parties also base the counter argument propagating the incidence of corruption and other deficiencies. In a sense, the propaganda or political value of panchayats is more pronounced than their developmental fecundity. Such daily dose of propaganda imbues and embeds the basic information about the structure and purpose of panchayats in the psyche of the general villagers.

Whether one is empathetic or antagonistic, no one can avoid or ignore Gram Panchayat, the most intimate and imposing panchayat tier. Almost every villager has to come and avail few of its authorisation functions like registration of life and death, income certificate for admission to educational institutions and the certificates for other official requirements. Thus, rural people get acquainted with the functions and functionaries, at least partially. As a result of constant harping by political parties, the imperative of panchayat and free flowing comments from fellow others, most of the villagers are somewhat familiar with the structure and activities of GP.

However, the responses relating to the nature and importance of Sansad are somewhat at variance with their subsequent responses, possibly an offshoot of party propaganda. Three specific questions were posed to the villagers: whether Sansad is an important institution for the villagers or not, who should receive importance in Sansad meeting and whether personal or community problems should be placed in the meeting. Majority reported that Sansad is "very important" for the villagers, only villagers—not Pradhan, GP members—ought to get importance and collective concerns should be placed in Sansad meetings. When countered why then were they not going to the meetings and asserting their importance or why many of them were demanding individual level benefits, many fumbled to furnish a strong defence. However, as regards the individual centric demand, some villagers put forth impregnable logic: "individual level problems and demands must receive due consideration because they constitute the social demands. And the proportion of social demands would only shrink when individual level demands are assuaged". At the same time, "only after alleviating my immediate requirement, I can think of and go for collective demands".

Prelude to Meetings

The Sansad and Sabha meetings are normally held and this is an improvement compared to many other states. The dates of Sansad meetings are fixed technically by the ordinary meeting of GP. In practice the decision depends on many considerations: preparedness of GP as in completing the reports to be placed in the meeting, the nature of ongoing development schemes, possibility of fund release and assessment of the political situation by party leaders. In some CPM dominated GP the decision about holding the meeting was first taken by the *Pradhan Shayahak Committee*, an informal committee, and then formally presented to and passed by GP. The dates of Sansad meeting are fixed on ward basis. The convenience of the Pradhan, GP officials rather than ward members and villagers happens to be decisive. For Sabha meeting, the date is either pre-fixed—somewhere 31 December every year—or is decided following the same procedure for Sansad.

After deciding the dates, advance notice is publicised through various means such as placing it on the notice board of GP, public announcement and sending printed leaflets to households. Somewhere GP members also inform the villagers accordingly and party leaders play an important role in information dissemination.[2] Wide publicity is generally arranged and villagers get to know the date and other information about the meeting. One-fourth of the respondent could, therefore, get the information of Sansad meetings well in advance (Figure 3.1).

Along with the notice of meetings no agenda items are generally mentioned. Legally, the half-yearly and yearly Sansad meetings will have different items for discussion and recommendation but the prescribed agenda is rarely followed. Even in the proceedings of the meetings, if available in GP office, one will hardly notice the agenda of the meeting. Generally, it is the placement of GP reports, proposal for few development programmes and names of the already selected beneficiaries that can be observed in Sansad and Sabha meetings.

The legal stipulations concerning the time slots—May and November for Sansad and December for Sabha—are not always adhered in many GPs including the sample ones. For instance, in Malighati GP, the annual Sansad for 2008 was held during last week of August in 2 wards and first week of September in remaining 11 wards. In Andaran Fulbari II, annual Sansad was held during last week of August in 3 wards. The legal framework is flouted reportedly for one compelling reason. When GP remains understaffed, or its officials are otherwise preoccupied, finalisation of reports and list of beneficiaries cannot be completed. In such case the meetings invariably get deferred. After 2008 panchayat elections, Sansad and Sabha meetings were not held in many GPs across the state because the newly formed GP Board could not get the required information or it could not compile the reports. At the same time, when the meeting is adjourned for lack of quorum, it is not always reconvened after 7 days. When a Sansad meeting could not be held in a ward for whatever reason, there is a tendency to hold that in the subsequent month, designating it as one special Sansad.

One worrisome trend is to hold Sansad meeting in one day for more than one ward or by clubbing 2–3 wards together. In Malighati GP, for instance, the half-yearly Sansad for 2008 was held for two wards each on 21st, 22nd, 25th and 26th and for 3 wards on 24th November. Almost similar incidence was observed in Andaran Fulbari I GP during 2007. When more than one Sansads are held in one day, the Pradhan tends to devote less time and energy, thereby undermining the objective of the meeting. When more than one ward is bunched together (as found in sample adjacent GPs) the very purpose of the meeting gets lost.

The usual time of Sansad meeting is 3–4 PM and the venue is one primary school compound (for Sabha the office premise of GP). But most meetings start late, at about 5–6 PM. They commence late because the Pradhan or people come late. The ward level GP member could be seen searching (sometimes frantically) for and requesting people to come. The Pradhan comes late, only after fulfilling official duties or party programmes.

Sabha meeting is presided over by the Pradhan but the same is not always the case for Sansad. The Pradhan does not invariably attend and preside over Sansad meetings. When more than one Sansad is held in one day s/he may skip one and when urgent official or political engagement comes up s/he cannot make it. Sansad meetings last for about 2 hours. The Pradhan, GP officials, somewhere political leaders sit in the chair arranged on the dais and villagers sit on the ground facing the dais and dignitaries. The use of microphone is common for Sabha but not for Sansad.

The attendance of the participants is collected all through the meeting generally by one group D staff of GP. The records of attendance and proceedings are casually recorded and such registers are poorly maintained. In the attendance registers, if available in GP office, the date, time and signatures of participants will be found missing in many instances. In a few cases, only a short note on important points discussed and delved will be found jotted down, often in a separate sheet of paper. The proceedings of the meetings are seldom written ad verbatim.

What GP records can at the most divulge is a synoptic and not comprehensive picture of such meetings. All these authenticate how casually GP treats such meetings. If GPs do not maintain the records of the meetings satisfactorily, the scenario at the state level is no better either.[3]

Participation in Assembly Meetings

The participation of the members in Sansad and Sabha meetings has two distinct yet interrelated dimensions: formal or figurative and proactive or substantive in the sense of submitting own views and influencing the decision and outcome of the meeting. Formal participation is symbolic or passive, having no bearing on the meeting in tangible terms except achieving quorum. Both the dimensions of participation have been investigated in the subsequent paragraphs. Given the high degree of awareness and regularity of meetings, it can be assumed that villagers are both enthused about and active in those meetings. Survey data and information authenticate that they do attend the meetings, at least ceremonially.

Total 31 per cent respondents had attended Sansad meetings, either one or two during the year of interview. In five GPs the attendance rates were over 35 per cent. In four GPs, especially in Dadpur of Murshidabad, the rates were not on the higher side. Both in absolute number and percentage terms, slightly fewer people (26%) reported their attendance in Sabha meeting. In three GPs, the attendance rates for Sabha meetings were higher than Sansad. While in Dadpur no respondents participated, the participation rates in Sabha were relatively marginal in two GP of Birbhum district (Table 3.1).

In fact the attendance rates for Sabha meetings are fairly high particularly when the stipulated quorum is only 5 per cent, when the venue of meeting is not nearer to the residence of most of the villagers, when the time of meeting is generally late evening, when the attendance of people is declining steadily throughout the state and when Sabha is virtually losing out to Sansad in terms of powers and authority.

Table 3.1

Attendance in Sansad and Sabha Meetings

	Sansad Meetings			*Sabha Meetings*		
GP	*Yes*	*No*	*Total*	*Yes*	*No*	*Total*
1*	16 (35)	30 (65)	46	17 (37)	29 (63)	46
2	14 (39)	22 (61)	36	15 (42)	21 (58)	36
3	20 (40)	30 (60)	50	18 (36)	32 (64)	50
4	17 (34)	33 (66)	50	21(42)	29 (58)	50
5	16 (36)	29 (64)	45	9 (20)	36 (80)	45
6	9 (21)	33 (79)	42	9 (21)	33 (79)	42
7	21 (43)	28 (57)	49	19 (39)	30 (61)	49
8	3 (9)	31 (91)	34	0 (0)	34 (100)	34
9	9 (20)	37 (80)	46	3 (97)	43 (93)	46
10*	10 (26)	28 (74)	38	4 (11)	34 (89)	38
Total	135 (31)	301 (69)	436	115 (26)	321 (74)	436

* Name of Gram Panchayats: 1. Andaran Fulbari I (Cooch Behar), 2. Andaran Fulbari II (Cooch Behar), 3. Golgram (Paschim Midnapur), 4. Malighati (Paschim Midnapur), 5. Majigram (Burdwan), 6. Kshigram (Burdwan), 7. Shaktipur (Murshidabad), 8. Dadpur (Murshidabad), 9. Karidhya (Birbhum), 10. Tilpara (Birbhum). This sequence has been followed in subsequent Tables.

Figures in parentheses indicate rounded-off percentage.

Figure 3.2

Duration of Presence in Sansad and Sabha Meetings

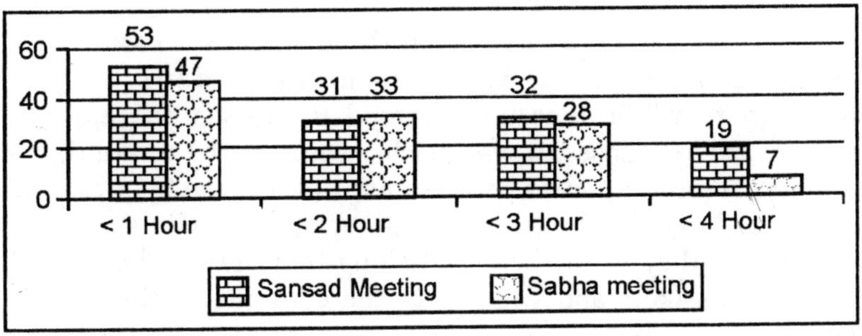

The respondents stayed in the meetings for a considerable period (Figure 3.2). Notwithstanding the total duration of the meeting and the exact time when members came in, majority of the members reportedly stayed in meetings for more than one hour—less than one hour presence was marked for 39 per cent in Sansad and 41 per cent in Sabha. Majority respondents, presumably, stayed almost to the end of the meeting and the vast majority did not leave just after registering their presence.

The reported attendance rates for Sansad and Sabha do not conform to other survey results available for West Bengal and even to the published government figures. The average rates obtained from village survey were 12 per cent for Ghatak (2002) and 19 per cent for Kumar (2006).[4] Figures released by the department of Panchayat and Rural Development divulge an average rate of 11 per cent for Sansad and just 5 per cent for Sabha meetings over the years. District-wise public figures for two Sansad meetings during 2002 show that the average rates for the districts taken as sample were far less than what the survey results disclose: 18 per cent in Cooch Behar, 12 per cent in Murshidabad, 15 per cent in Paschim Midnapur, 13 per cent in Bardhaman and only 8 per cent (below quorum) in Birbhum district.[5]

Data collected from the official records of the sample GPs also corroborate that people's attendance for Sansad and Sabha meetings was lower than the survey results. In Malighati GP 21 per cent (34% male and 7% female) attended the annual Sansad meeting during 2008 and the rate in Golgram GP was 25 per cent (32% male and 18% female) during 2007 annual Sansad.

Was the clear hiatus between the survey results and other studies and reports a case where respondents tried to satisfy the interviewer? While it is unwarranted to suspect the authenticity of the responses, it was neither easy for the respondents to manufacture responses because many other related questions were asked: where the meeting was held, what was the time, with whom they went there, how long they stayed there, who were the speakers and what were the contents of the speech delivered.

One probable reason accounting for the divergence may be that we had ended up interviewing mainly those villagers who attended those meetings, a possibility arising out of non-stratified sampling. Perhaps more concrete as well as convincing reason relates to a higher concentration of labourers in the sample and their propensity to attend those meetings. The landless and marginal farmers constitute' overwhelming majority of participants in GS meetings not only in West Bengal but also in other states. In the sample, the labourers comprise the single largest class (30% of total) and for this reason the proportion of participation has increased perceptibly. In fact, labourers alone accounted for 30 per cent Sansad and 47 per cent Sabha participants.

Notwithstanding the higher rate of participation, more than 2/3 of total respondents did not or could not participate in those meetings. Regarding the reasons for the absence, the responses reveal few broad patterns: illness, occupational or work pressures, family preoccupations, personal engagements and out-migration for wage employment. Only a handful did not know the exact date of the meeting and the venue was inconvenient and controvertible for a few.

Kalpana Hembram, one middle aged ST women from Malighati GP summed up the predicaments of the labourers: "being one agricultural labourer, I have to go to different places and villages for searching and doing subsistence works. I cannot always stay in the village for all the days. When I find work in other villages, I sometimes stay there. Therefore, it is not possible to attend Sansad, even when I have the inclination".

It was pressure of domestic work and inconvenient time schedule of Sansad and Sabha meetings that proved deterrent for womenfolk. Domestic chores coupled with the extensive wage earning activities were obtruding particularly for ST and SC women. As one ST woman labourer of Golgram GP pointed out: "because of insurmountable domestic work together with eyebrows of family males, I thought it desirable to give Sansad meeting a go by". For the younger women in particular and middle aged women in general, the abstention stemmed mainly from the inexpedient time of the meetings.

Most respondents had not overtly expressed their disinclination or indicated the triviality of Sansad meeting. However, few women did not have any idea about Sansad and Sabha. Joytsa Bagdi, one middle aged housewife from Karidhya GP put it rather bluntly: "what is Sansad? I am not aware of it. Neither anyone appraised me about it nor did anybody request me to go there".

Only two respondents raised pointed questions about the sanctity and worth of Sansad; "what is the use of it? It has no positive outcome. Only lecture is delivered and grand programmes are announced repeatedly. But all these are for public consumption only as there is no follow up action of what has publicly been pronounced". Moreover, "the discussion revolves basically around (revised) BPL list which is not the concern of everybody".

Few older respondents had expressed their dissatisfaction with the working of Sansad and with the way panchayats were being run. Some of them attended Sansad meeting, drew attention of GP members to some urgent issues like removal of garbage and need for sewerage and when those were not taken up in due course, they became disillusioned and refrained from attending subsequent meetings. Some older villagers, incidentally, conveyed their disapproval of high degree of politicisation and lack of morality in panchayat decisions and works. They were probably caught in the cross-fires of generation gaps and they could not cope with or tolerate new idioms of panchayat politics.

The specific reasons why respondents attended those meetings are somewhat curt, evasive and not as categorical or convincing as the reasons for absence. Nobody attended meetings out of curiosity or intending to see the nature of discussion. And this is comprehensible because those meetings are being held for years and villagers have, in general, gained some idea about those. Neither their responses demonstrated that they had attended meetings with the motive to formulate village development plan, to get information about what development programmes would be undertaken in the ward, or to castigate GP members for the failure to extend civic or infrastructural facilities or to seek personal or family centred benefits.

Their common refrains were: "we have to go" (*jeete habee tai*), "as many other fellow villagers go" (*sabai jaaye*), panchayat member or party functionaries "requested to attend", or to bring the deprivation (exclusion from BPL list) to the notice and seek redress from the Pradhan and panchayat members, etc. Only a minuscule sub-section, obviously politically active ones, echoed what is claimed at the party platform: Sansad and Sabha are the popular assemblies; villagers are to attend for their own sake and interest, to strengthen GP efforts as by lending support to the 'pro-poor' and 'comprehensive village development'.[6]

The disclosed reasons occasioning their participation in such meetings allude to the fact that villagers attended more to abide by the request of panchayat members and party functionaries. As they themselves are the supporters of the party that GP members represent, they found it peremptory to come to meetings. Equally, they could not possibly ignore or defy the request of panchayat and party functionaries as that could have many negative consequences. The villagers have to depend on party leaders for many contingencies and the compliance with the request would express the political solidarity that can beget reciprocity as and when required. Together with the political consideration or compulsion, also implicit was the demonstrative effects. As the neighbours belonging to the same party are going, 'why-not-me' might have also influenced the villagers.

Participation might have been another variant of evening gossiping or relaxing incidence. In the evening, villagers have very little work and they do not have access to entertainment. In earlier years the social life of male villagers centred on discussion houses (*Baithakkhana*) where they assembled, passed the evening time by playing cards, gossiping and discussing. Such informal system—fallen into disuse from 1970 (Rudd, 2003: 153)—has transformed into gathering in one convenient location such as tea stall, grocer's shop where they try to relax a bit by meeting and gossiping with fellow others. Incidentally and crucially, such informal gathering centres have emerged as the fountainhead where the perception of the villagers is formed or reformed and where few core issues of village politics are shaped or reshaped.[7] Attending Sansad-like meeting may be a shift of the location of such gathering for a day.

What is explicit from the responses is the irreconcilability between villagers' expressed assumption and how they act or work up. While they tend to regard Sansad as their own forum, they do not participate, overtly motivated by an articulated desire to effectuate such assumption. Implicitly, Sansad and Sabha are, to the majority villagers, an extension arm of GP and not the popular or plebeian institution where they themselves are the masters, where they would provide all the inputs, dictate the development decision and guide the implementation process of GP level schemes.

One pertinent issue is the extent of involvement of the family members of the respondents in those meetings. Do the participants represent the family members or can they do so? Survey data available for Sansad meetings divulge that family members of 22 per cent respondents—like wife, husband, brother, sister—attended meetings and total 33 per cent respondents discussed Sansad issues with their family members.

There has been a tendency to consider the participation of family head as the participation of the entire family members. If the number of family so represented by the family head is taken into consideration, the usual lower rate of attendance will multiply. As one argument goes: "voters from the same village are often members of the same extended family or close-knit social network. A person attending the meetings (often the household head) is likely to represent the views of more than one voter, and so in terms of effective popular participation, the attendance rate may appear lower than it really is" (Ghatak et al., 2002: 50).

The assumption that the family head represents the views and opinions of the family members as well, needs to be considered cautiously. When one member demands individual or family centred benefits, the wish of other family members and the impact of the benefits on the economic condition of the family may be obvious. But when it is a community issue like selection of development scheme or election of members to a committee, etc., does (and can) the view of the family head embody the wishes of other family members? If so, will it not then furnish a strong handle to particularly perpetuate the marginality of women members in those meetings and ultimately negate the liberal ethos of individual as the basic political and social unit?

Deliberation in Meetings

More than mere holding a meeting and attendance of a certain number of members, critically crucial is the incidence, frequency and nature of the discussion held, the impulse of deliberation on the outcome of the meeting and the ostensible motive moulding the participation of the members as these facets will indicate how the democratic space has been used, how articulation and aggregation of public priorities have been made, how accountability has been enforced and, in a word, how successful the meeting has really been.

Deliberation in both Sansad and Sabha meetings, almost evenly, follows a set pattern and it is in this respect the meetings are structured. The Pradhan customarily delivers a long speech and GP officials read out various reports—all accounting for no less than 3/4 time of meeting.[8] The ward members do not always speak in the Sansad, more so when they are women. The Pradhan talks about the overall policy of the party s/he represents, the objective and importance of panchayats, Sansad and Sabha as the case may be, major development schemes already undertaken or being mulled, pressing problems of GP areas and of course NREGS. GP officials present reports such as Administrative Report, Audit and Accounts and Budget. Somewhere (as in Bardhaman) few party leaders, not formally involved with GP, also address the meeting and their points touch party policy and development works. Only after completion of those lectures are villagers invited to place their point of view and they do speak out, though in far lesser number.

Survey data reveal that around 2/3 of total participants in Sansad and Sabha remained passive in the sense that they never said anything in the meeting. Conversely, 10 per cent of total respondents had spoken regularly and 25 per cent occasionally or rarely in Sansad meetings (Table 3.2). The number of those who spoke was indeed trivial in absolute figure. A statistical riddle creeps in the disaggregated analysis (as the unit size is widely uneven). In those GPs where least people attended Sansad in absolute number, the percentage figures for those who at any rate spoke in those GPs become quite high—when only two villagers said something, the figure shoots up as high as 67 per cent in percentage terms.

Around 33 per cent of total respondents attending Sabha meetings had spoken, none at all in Dadpur though (Table 3.3). Despite the statistical equivocation, in four GPs more than five persons and more than 30 per cent expressed their point of view. The 50 per cent figure for Tilpara actually implies speaking by only two members out of total four who attended. It needs emphasis that those members who spoke in Sansad did not necessarily speak in the Sabha. In majority cases, two different sets of members spoke out in two types of meetings. However, the proportion of public speaking in Sansad and Sabha seems to be higher compared to what other reports for West Bengal obliquely assert.

Table 3.2

Types of Public Speaking in Sansad Meeting

GP	*Regularly*	*Rarely*	*Never*	*Total*
1*	0	4 (25)	12 (75)	16
2	0	2 (14)	12 (86)	14
3	1 (5)	3 (15)	16 (80)	20
4	2 (12)	4 (24)	11 (64)	17
5	1 (6)	2 (13)	13 (81)	16
6	4 (44)	2 (22)	3 (33)	9
7	2 (10)	9 (43)	10 (47)	21
8	0	2 (67)	1 (33)	3
9	1 (11)	3 (33)	5 (56)	9
10*	2 (20)	3 (30)	5 (50)	10
Total	13 (10)	34 (25)	88 (65)	135

*GP names as cited earlier. Figures in parentheses indicate rounded-off percentage.

Table 3.3

Public Speaking in Sabha Meeting

	Types of Speaking		
GP	*Yes*	*No*	*Total*
1*	6 (35)	11 (65)	17
2	4 (27)	11 (73)	15
3	6 (33)	12 (67)	18
4	7 (33)	14 (67)	21
5	2 (22)	7 (78)	9
6	3 (33)	6 (67)	9
7	7 (37)	12 (63)	19
8	0	0	0
9	1 (33)	2 (67)	3
10	2 (50)	2 (50)	4
Total	38 (33)	77 (67)	115

* GP names as cited earlier. Figures in parentheses indicate rounded off percentage.

It should be mentioned that the type of speaking by the villagers in those meetings was certainly contrasting to what GP members and officials did. Generally, it was not akin to formal speaking for a length of time or covering different aspects or delving one issue in depth or with formal address to the audience. Rather, it was casual, like standing up, say something for a while and not more than that.

Respondents reportedly raised many issues in the meetings which, in descending order of the frequency are as follows: road repair, road construction, omission of names from BPL list, IAY selection, job card and works under NREGS, electricity including street light, drinking water, provision for drainage, irrigation, prevention of flood and river erosion, proper distribution of mini-kit, ration card, health centre and burning ghat. Surely, the subject matters varied depending upon the prevailing infrastructural and developmental conditions in the respective GPs. However, new construction and repair of road, BPL, IAY, NREGS, electricity and drinking water were common issues across those GPs.

Worth pondering is whether the issues raised by members in the meetings were personal or community concerns, even when the dividing line between the two is very thin and often overlapping. Majority of the issues raised seem to have community orientation—road, electricity, drinking water. What is intermittent is that the respondents were more motivated by their individual or family level predicaments and perception—dilapidated road condition preventing easy movement, flood destroying yield, drinking water supply for avoiding iron-infested water from tube-well.

Oft repeated assertion is that the political parties, particularly CPM, keep constant control over panchayat members and panchayat decision-making, probably inevitable for political panchayats as in West Bengal. Is the similar tethering observable over the public speaking in Sansad meetings? Though villagers are unlikely to confess, particularly to the outsiders, about the directives of party leaders over their voice, one study (Corbridge et al., 2003) has unearthed the intense extent of party reign over submission of issues in Sansad forum.

From the survey two specific types of party control over public speaking in those meetings have come to the fore: one direct and other discreet. For a few respondents, the tight lid over their points was consciously and directly attempted. Few respondents having the keen desire to raise certain issues had to budge when local level party leaders instructed them not to put across those in open meeting. And such an exercise is not amazing because if the public outlet or public outburst is not held in leash and if general people are allowed unfettered scope to place a long list of demands, express discontent or lambaste the failures of panchayats, that will be embarrassing for the GP members and detesting for the party leaders as this will bear out the hollowness of the claim of advancements and will entice other villagers to go against the party policy and decrees of party leaders.

The issues having general nature and common character are preferred for presentation in the forum of Sansad. Such common concerns of the villagers are pursued so as to publicly prove how concerned the leadership is with the woes of ordinary people. And the opportunity is skilfully used to explain the strategy and endeavour of the ruling leadership. Ananta Das, an agricultural labourer from Karidhya put the issue in wider perspective: "Sansad meetings are held as per the consideration and exigency of the ruling party. The meeting is dominated by the party leaders (including GP members) and is used to garner and retain political support base".

Whether the points and issues raised by the participants in the meetings have been considered by and finally incorporated in the resolution of the meeting is one crucial indicator of the tangible aspect of participation, as this will authenticate the influence, success of the public speaking, the extent of public input to the decision-making process of GP and this will also evince the worth and utility of such meetings.

Out of total 47 respondents who spoke in Sansad, 62 per cent felt that their points had been considered or accepted in the meeting and the rest were either uncertain or expressed non-compliance. Apparently, the information in the Table 3.4 attests an ample extent of public dimensions in the outcome of Sansad meeting and by extension, in the development decisions of GP. However, the extent of acceptance of points is not as emboldening in absolute figure as it is in percentage terms. While in one GP no one reported acceptance, in two other GPs the number ranged in between 5–6 and in five others it varied in the range of 1–3.

Many respondents might have been convinced about the consideration and acceptance of their view and demands, but more unequivocal is the fact that this information does not offer enough scope for going gaga. One apparently innocuous practice (strategy!) tends to have struck at the roots of public demands and the process of democratic decentralisation. Whatever the members had voiced or demanded in the public fora was indeed heard by the dignitaries present at the dais. Those public concerns were not entirely disregarded or deflected. Most of those were verbally responded mainly by the Pradhan. By bunching the public points into few broad groups like BPL, electricity the response was either an oral promise to consider those in future occasion, as and when scheme/fund will be available or an express inability of GP (because of lack of authority, resource) to meet or redress the demands or grievances. By and large, such oral responses might have impressed the respondents about the acceptance of their points. Otherwise they could not have been so certain.

Table 3.4

Reported Acceptance of Points Raised in Sansad Meeting

	Points Accepted or Not		
GP	*Yes*	*No*	*Total*
1*	3 (75)	1 (25)	4
2	2 (100)	0	2
3	3 (75)	1 (25)	4
4	4 (67)	2 (33)	6
5	1 (33)	2 (67)	3
6	5 (83)	1 (17)	6
7	6 (55)	5 (45)	11
8	0	2 (100)	2
9	2 (50)	2 (50)	4
10	3 (60)	2 (40)	5
Total	29 (62)	18 (38)	47

* GP names as cited earlier. Figures in parentheses indicate rounded off percentage.

The bottom line is that those public demands are seldom included in the resolution of Sansad. Indeed no resolution is formally and finally adopted and approved in most meetings. If the register for Sansad meeting is scanned, one is unlikely to find any formal resolution except, at best, a summery containing few observations like X raised question on BPL, Y on road condition, etc. Whatever is written as proceeding is enclosed afterwards, usually by one Group D staff during his free time and as per his ability, etc.[9] When the Sansad resolution is required for official purpose, the decisions are finalised at informal level—usually involving the Pradhan, ward member and local level party leaders. What are the final decisions pertaining to the ward areas are, almost as a rule, without the knowledge and approval of the general Sansad members, though few influential villagers may be privy to those. Those decisions are furnished to the appropriate authority and these are accepted as authentic.

We had the intension to investigate the extent and nature of popular demands concerning the village development plan and to determine how a GP was taking follow-up action either by incorporating those public points into formal decision/action plan of GP or initiating the works proper. In this way the association between the public initiatives and the functioning of the democratic institution could have been explored empirically. But the objective was cut short by the very absence of Sansad resolution in true sense and lack of clear linkage between public priority and activities of GP. At least in those three GPs where the proceedings of Sansad meeting has been recorded, there is no concrete evidence evincing that at least some decision or a broad framework has actually originated from the meeting after threadbare discussion, deliberation, dithering and with the knowledge and approval of the participants (Appendix 4).

One may regard this as one deliberate strategy aimed at retaining the final decision-making power of GP members or as a mockery debasing the very purpose of the popular assembly. Yet, there are some practical difficulties involved in taking final decision in a Sansad meeting. The priorities and demands of villagers are surely variegated and contrasting—some of which like electricity, drinking water are also beyond the functional jurisdiction of GP. It is not unproblematic to hammer out unanimity or consensus in an open and occasional forum. About 2-hour time span is yet another constraint. Nor are the managerial skill and accommodative temperament always available among GP members. Leaving aside the more problematic personal benefit scheme, the selection of location for a road construction project, for instance, is more likely to involve claims and counter claims. Some may demand it nearer to the house, some may be unwilling to part with land and some may question the very rationale of kuchha road and may insist on pucca road, etc. Given the time available and conflicting claims, few pertinent as well as practical issues are: how the

Sansad will arrive at a consensus, who will take the lead, who will budge, who will gain, will the GP members voluntarily concede final decision-making power to the people. Dissemination of information, consultation with and ascertaining public priority and demand is one thing but taking final and binding decision out of many alternatives is quite another and often complex task.

Final decision-making relating to any development issue is not as simple as is generally supposed. Many unobserved pulls, personal and political equations and dynamics are involved. It is, in simplistic terms, the league of the Pradhan, ward level GP member and influential party leaders who finally take decision. It may be a travesty to popular voice but the reverse process is also fraught with time constraint, clash of interest, delay and procedural hassles including technical norms.

Perception and Preference of Beneficiaries

Right from the sixth five-year plan, the target oriented poverty alleviation and other centrally sponsored welfare programmes have intended to serve the target population and to satisfy the felt needs of the rural population without leakage and corruption. The growing realisation is that mere representative institutions are not suffice and direct public involvement in decision-making is indispensable. In this context the discernable trend is the increasing emphasis on open selection of eligible and appropriate persons for the existing schemes and programmes by the villagers themselves. Incidentally, the beneficiary selection is the most common function of GS in all states and here GS is fervently expected to emerge as the magic bullet that can obviate undue manipulation and can extend succour to the most deserving target group population.

Regarding the questions how many respondents received benefits of public schemes, which forum they used for securing the benefit and what platform they intended to avail for getting benefits in future occasion, few broad patterns emerge. About 27 per cent respondents had received benefits from GP level schemes, mostly IAY, OAP. In some GPs few families got more than one type of benefits while none could lay hand to in one

GP of Murshidabad. Though Sansad has got the final say in picking out those who would be shortlisted for receiving scheme benefits, the responses reveal that what is legally mandated is not always factual in practice. Most villagers did not place the demand for benefits in Sansad meeting: total 85 per cent. Vast majority preferred the elected ward members or the Pradhan—53 per cent and 24 per cent respectively (Table 3.5). In one-half of total GPs, Sansad forum was not availed at all. In two GPs the demands were placed either to the panchayat members or to party leaders. In two other GPs most members placed the demand to the Pradhan and not to the ward level panchayat member. The information perhaps point to who really controlled the decision-making in those GPs. Anyway, the marginal role of Sansad in selecting beneficiaries is vindicated. And why this is so has been elaborated in the last Chapter.

Table 3.5

Panchayat Benefits Demanded From

GP	No. of Recipients	Person/Institution				
		Sansad	Panchayat Member	Pradhan	Panchayat + Pradhan	Party Leader
1*	19	17**	59**	17**	6**	0**
2	17	13	60	13	13	0
3	15	8	92	0	0	0
4	20	56	44	0	0	0
5	16	0	100	0	0	0
6	8	0	17	83	0	0
7	16	7	0	93	0	0
8	0	0	0	0	0	0
9	4	0	0	0	0	100
10	9	0	43	44	13	0
Total	116	15	53	24	4	4

* GP names as cited earlier.

** Figures in rounded-off percentage to column 2.

Furthermore, total 48 per cent (some already in receipt) did have the longing for scheme benefits (Table 3.6). If the 27 per cent who have already received benefits are excluded from those having no aspiration, it would tentatively imply that around 3/4 of respondents have the aspiration for benefits and the participation of the majority members in Sansad meetings is somewhat related to such hankering. Regarding the forum they intended to use for getting benefit in future, few absorbing dimensions manifest when the information of Table 3.5 are also taken into account. Slightly more number of villagers compared to earlier occasion—a gain of 4 percentage points—would now opt for Sansad. About 3/4 respondents would prefer Sansad in Malighati, a GP where more than 1/2 respondents earlier used Sansad for placing demands for benefits. But in five other GPs no respondents would go through the route of Sansad. Furthermore, the Pradhan would receive lesser preference and the importance of the party leaders would leap by twofold

It can be inferred that the villagers sought to use the forum that was quickly and materially rewarding for securing the benefits. They might have overlooked Sansad because they perceived that positive outcome is unlikely to come through it or because they found it expedient to approach the dispenser directly. Deductively, the decision-making centre varied in those GPs; somewhere it was the Pradhan, or party leaders and somewhere the ward level GP members were not purely a push-over. Moreover, the wielders of decision-making power were also amenable or open to public demands: otherwise people would not have approached the Pradhan and party leaders. The contrasting decision-making process in GPs also tends to indicate the disparate political culture existing therein, possibly conditioned by the party position in the GP, the orientation and ability of GP members and party functionaries. Overall, it gets credence that the decisive and clinching role of Sansad in selecting beneficiaries for public schemes is more a pious hope than a reality, more phoney than actual, at least in the sample GPs.

Table 3.6

To Whom Respondents Would Like to Place Demand for Benefit

GP	*No. of Respondents*	*Sansad*	*Panchayat Member*	*Pradhan*	*Panchayat + Pradhan*	*Party Leader*
1*	5	20**	20**	20**	40**	0**
2	7	43	29	14	14	0
3	36	17	83	0	0	0
4	37	73	19	8	0	0
5	27	0	93	7	0	0
6	21	0	5	95	0	0
7	10	0	20	50	0	30
8	24	0	66	17	0	17
9	21	0	67	0	0	33
10	23	13	57	17	0	13
Total	211	19	53	19	1	8

* Name of GP as cited earlier.
** Figures in rounded-off percentage to column 2.

Sansad and Right to Work

A brief mention about the role of Sansad in regard to the NREGS may be in order.[10] As per the National Rural Employment Guarantee Scheme, West Bengal, 2006 Sansad has been assigned primary responsibility for providing assured works and for making the scheme a success. Tersely, Sansad in its annul meeting in November will discuss and finally approve project proposals on a priority basis and submit those to GP for finalising annual Action Plan for next year. The role of Sansad extends to sensitisation efforts, assessment of possible demand for works and passing scheme proposals for the ward concerned. GP will compile the scheme proposals received from all Sansads within the territorial jurisdiction and, together with other proposals covering more than one ward, will forward the action plan to the Panchayat Samity.

Indeed, in many Sansad meetings NREGS figured prominently. The Pradhans explained the scheme guideline, criteria for scheme proposals and the problems encountered by GP while formulating work proposals and implementing the scheme. Many participants also demanded works and more work opportunities under the scheme. The discussion in the Sansad was centred, basically, on the public demands for works and the expressed inability of GP to cater to or satisfy the public demands by undertaking more schemes and providing additional works. Worth noting is the fact that no effort to assess the possible demand for works, seeking proposals for scheme works from the general participants or placing those for discussion and authorisation was either reported by the respondents or buttressed by the participant observation.

This is not to say that no work under NREGS had been made available. One half of total respondents registered themselves and 42 per cent of them also got works, a high proportion in a state having trembling track records.[11] Though the nature of works varied across GPs, the major activities respondents undertook were: road repair and construction, earth works, pond digging, cleaning of drain and weed along road, repair of culverts and bundhs, boulder carrying and spread of *murrum*.

Rather than any positive as such, few specific problems come to the fore. The estimation of possible demands for works from the ward members and concrete proposals for project works including the nature and location are not originating from Sansad forum, a clear departure from the scheme guidelines. This is not to deny the comprehensive annual Action Plans of GPs that contain inventory of projects. Such NREGS action plans, ironically the only plan a GP is presently preparing, are submitted to Panchayat Samity and district authority and a huge fund is being sanctioned. When such project proposals are not setting off from the Sansad, how are these being prioritised and finalised? Possibly, the picking and choosing is done by GP members in active collaboration with the Pradhan, GP officials and party functionaries.

From administrative standpoint, the NREGS guidelines and scheme criteria are posing problems and constricting the scope to make optimal use of the scheme, certainly disproportionate to the public demands. The scheme does not offer free hand to GPs, it instead prescribes specific activities which are not possible or viable in every GP. Because of lack of sufficient number of shelving of projects, few strategies are being followed so that people cannot invoke the guarantee clause and they cannot prove that they have been denied works within 15 days of demand.

When the wage rate for NREGS works is lower than the prevailing market rate and when the wage payment is delayed for months, many people may not opt for the works. Even if they do, workers may be subjected to avoidable exploitation. As one respondent summed it up; "if I work as a helper of a mason, I will get ₹ 90–100 per day. The NREGS works, after so much procedural hassles and parley with others, can offer me just ₹ 70 and when I will receive the payment is uncertain. If I can get work fairly regularly, why should I go for the NREGS works?"

Despite the claim that transparency and accountability has for the first time been built into this public programmes, the incidence of manipulation and corruption has not melted away entirely. The allegation, particularly in Malighati GP of Paschim Midnapur, is that the "party leaders and panchayat functionaries are playing a selfish and partisan role. The registration and distribution of job cards are not transparent and need-based. The works are mired in non-transparency, controversy and fraud".

Cultural Show in Sabha Meetings

A colourful cultural show is commonly held in Sabha meetings—nowhere in Sansad—where after completion of the official business different events like singing and dancing are staged by local artists catering to the local taste and tradition (i.e., folk songs like *kabi ghan, baul ghan, Bhawaiya*). This sort of programme, it is claimed, entrenches the attendance rates, provides entertainment and helps preservation of local cultural tradition.

There has been argument for such cultural shows. As the villagers usually show lukewarm response to GS meetings, some sort of incentive to arouse their interest may not be unjustified. Diwankar Committee (GoI, 1963: 48) recommended for recreational programme or film show immediately after the meeting. In West Bengal such programme has received much ado. "The meetings have been more successful where the gram panchayat and the parties have taken initiative in synchronising these with the cultural programmes in tune with the local traditions. The modern institutional assemblies need to be tuned with the natural rhythm" (Datta et al., 2000: 47).

Before arriving at definite conclusion about the worth of such cultural show, it is necessary to gauge the perception and preference of the villagers themselves. In this context, the responses regarding the question—whether they like exclusively the cultural programme, the deliberation of the meeting or like both equally—reveal that 27 per cent of total clearly favoured the show, 20 per cent expressed their enmity and 17 per cent liked both the show and the deliberation. Altogether 36 per cent did not respond to the questions. Taking non-response into account, it gets vindicated that more than 1/2 villagers did not have clear preference for the show. There may be another angle to the approval or animosity. Those villagers anyway are attached to the performing artists (e.g., parents, relatives) might have supported and those not so connected were abhorrent.

Without disparaging the effects of the cultural show on the increased attendance rate and the entertainment impact on the otherwise 'mundane' village life, few points require emphasis. Sabha meeting is not just one cultural show, it has many other important objectives. If and when the show gets priority, the efficacy and worth of Sabha is bound to suffer. West Bengal may not have taken the cue from the recommendation of Diwankar Committee but has rather been compelled, in the face of public apathy, to devise such show as a strategy to swell signatures. This common practice throughout the state seems one indirect enticement to attract more people, an irony for an important village forum. Furthermore, each GP expends few thousand rupees from its own tax revenue for conducting the show. That the expenditure could have been utilised for other productive purposes, may not be one dismissive contention.

Social Background and Participation

An effort is made in this section to find out association, if any, between the socio-economic background variables and the incidence of participation of the respondents in Sansad and Sabha meetings. This is expected to shed some light on how far the socio-economic attributes mould the perception and propel the participation and role performance of the assembly members.

In order to assess the impact of background variables on the participation of villagers, few socio-economic variables and participatory variables have been considered. Participatory variables are: attendance in both Sansad and Sabha meetings and types of speaking in those two types of meetings. Those dependent variables are supposed to have been induced by few independent 'stock variables' like gender, age, caste, education, landholding and occupation. Moreover, an additional endeavour has been to sneak a quick look at whether there are perceptible variations in participation of the members in terms of party affiliation and the geographical location of the sample GPs. To trace such relationship, the responses of respondents have been disaggregated and presented in a simple tabular format.

Background variable study may be common as well as easy for the political leadership but it is problematic for the village assembly members. In formal political institutions the ascriptive status of the incumbents plays a significant role as the leaders are to get party sponsorship, win majority support of the electorate and here the available positions are scanty, competition is intense and 'skill' based. In the village assembly, the participation is purely occasional and for a while. Here all the members are expected to participate and influence the course of the meeting. The general and open nature of participation makes the ascriptive status and other prerequisites more or less redundant. Moreover, the participation is either for securing personal benefit or for formulating village development plan, depending upon the thrust and operational ambit of a GP. As the stake involves either personal interest or community development, most members so concerned are likely to participate. The political leadership has also direct interest in ensuring large attendance of members as that would fulfil legal quorum as well as consolidate political support base. The assembly meeting is like the exercise of franchise during a polling day where the electorate are to cast ballot and where no specific condition, except the name in the electoral roll, is required.

Yet, participation in such meetings may not entirely be independent of background variables. As in many South Indian villages, Dalits are to sit in a designated place and they are not supposed to open their mouth in GS meetings. Moreover, one has to be quite informed, alert and vocal in saying something, voicing claims, criticising the performance of a development programme or suggesting alternative plan proposal. In the meeting the villagers are expected to comment, evaluate the ongoing scheme, at times to correct the course of activities or policy and even to confront the wishes of GP leadership. In this context background variables may play a part in influencing or determining the nature and course of the participation of the members of Sansad and Sabha.

Gender

Gender does play a role in shaping the perception, behavioural pattern and role performance of an individual in the socio-political process. While women in general have a subjugated social status, more so in traditional and rural societies, they find it very difficult to break into the political arena which is universally regarded as the male bastion. Though Indian women in rural areas have gained some visibility in the local governments due to the statutory reservation,[12] the egalitarian spirit is still to entrench evenly and squarely: the phenomenon of *bibi, beti brigade* and the statutory provision in some states prohibiting male companion of women panchayat members are just two examples of how extensive is the male domination.

Women's participation in village assemblies is ambivalent. If their responses are considered en block, it can be found that their participation in Sansad and Sabha meetings is not peripheral or subdued compared to male counterpart (Table 3.7). Women members participated in those meetings and spoke out almost at par with males. They also reported the acceptance of the issues they raised—29 per cent compared to 34 per cent for males, though one should take this information only at its face value as no formal resolution is adopted in those meetings. However, the perception that their points have been heeded or considered is likely to inspire them to attend and speak in subsequent meetings.

If the survey data in aggregate format indicate near absence of gender differentials and disprove the findings of many other research studies, a completely different scenario is obtained when that data are disaggregated GP-wise. Women's participation could have been really worse but for their participation in two GPs of Paschim Midnapur. If the figures of these two GPs are excluded from the overall responses, women's attendance would come down to only 12 per cent in Sansad meetings and just 9 per cent in Sabha meetings. Similarly, the speaking rates for Sansad would slump from 27 per cent to mere 13 per cent and for Sabha from 29 per cent to abysmal 8 per cent.

Golgram and Malighati GP of Paschim Midnapur had considerable presence of tribal population and tribal women of these GPs participated in relatively larger number. The basic reason was the momentary or migratory absence of family males for eking out livelihood. Surely, tribal women themselves were engaged in wage earning activities, generally doing labouring out of the village. During the day of meeting those tribal women present in the village had attended the Sansad and Sabha meetings and they also expressed their views and adversities. The less constricting social stigma compared to Hindu hierarchy and utter impoverishment might have influenced their participation and speaking. Incidentally, the educational level of those tribal women was really miserable, so also their husbands, though somewhat improved for their offspring. The abject economic and educational conditions and strenuous as well as uncertain occupation of the respondents may well be typical for other tribal population in the region and such deplorable conditions may have contributed to the recent tribal uprising and Maoist movement in vast stretches of the Paschim Midnapur district.

Age

In order to verify the influence of the background variable age, the respondents have been categorised into three broad age groups: low with less than 35 years of age, middle with 35–50 and high with more than 50 years. Total 94 (22%) respondents belong to the low-age group category, 216 (49%) to middle tier and 126 (29%) to high-age bracket.

Discernable is the feeble presence and infrequent speaking by the low age group members in Sansad and Sabha meetings (Table 3.7). Somewhat contradictory trends manifest in other groups. In Sansad meetings, middle age-group members participated more than the high age-group members, who, conversely, raised voices comparatively strongly and frequently. A reverse pattern is observed in Sabha meetings where the high age-group members had recorded a 10 percentage point lead in attendance over middle group, who scored over the high age-group in the sphere of public speaking.

Aged respondents are generally the bread winner, guardian and they also control other family members and represent the family interests. Being relatively better informed and mature, they know how and where to pursue the development issues and to demand benefits having bearing on family. Perhaps as a corollary to the maturity and family responsibility, they did speak in Sansad and Sabha meetings comparatively frequently.

The relatively shaken, though not entirely insignificant, participation of the younger people is not specifically because they are apolitical, oblivious to socio-political issues or unconcerned with the village problems. This phenomenon is more related to the very perception about PRIs, the subject matters of the meeting and the immediate preoccupations of the group individual family members. As long as the people come to Sansad meeting motivated by benefits and they clamour for scheme benefits, young villagers will tend to be less inclined or interested in the meetings. The house under IAY, mini-kit or bank loan is basically the concern of the family head. The fixation of the younger villagers is with how to get service, win contract, secure loan for entrepreneurship, etc. Unless and until Sansad and Sabha establish their mettle in community issues and village governance, younger generation will probably play truant.

Caste

In India caste significantly determines the function, the status, the opportunity as well as the handicaps for an individual. The political life is influenced by caste to a greater extent in rural areas than in the urban centres.[13] The caste system is, of course, undergoing radical changes, mainly due to the influence of electoral politics and reservation policy. In West Bengal caste system is said to be uniquely different, here it is supposed to be more or less a two-tier or bi-polar system. Moreover, caste system is said to have lost much of its force and ferocity in the state. Accordingly, there has been one discernable trend where caste variable is either ignored in the background study or two broad categories—SC, ST and other general caste—are employed in the analysis.

Total 157 (36%) respondents belong to SC, 51 (12%) to ST, 43 (10%) to Other Backward Classes (OBC), 13 (3%)to Muslim community and the rest 172 (39%) are from general caste, that is belonging to any other categories except the above.

Caste-wise break-up of survey data divulges that SC and ST people had participated in Sansad and Sabha meetings in greater number than any other single category (Table 3.7). The general caste members largely abstained from these meetings—87 per cent for Sansad and 83 per cent for Sabha. Participation rates for the OBC and Muslim community members were higher than the general caste members.

Table 3.7

*Socio-economic Background and Participation of the Respondents**

		Attended Sansad		Attended Sabha		Spoke in Sabha		Spoke in Sansad		
		Yes (135)	No (301)	Yes (115)	No (325)	Yes (38)	No (77)	Regu. (13)	Rarely (34)	Never (88)
Gender	Male (349)	31	69	27	73	34	66	10	27	63
	Female (87)	30	70	24	76	29	71	8	19	73
Age	High (126)	31	69	34	66	28	72	8	31	61
	Medium (216)	34	66	25	75	40	60	11	24	65
	Low (94)	23	77	20	80	26	74	9	18	73
Caste/Community	Gen (174)	13	87	17	83	55	45	13	52	35
	SC (157)	44	66	36	64	27	73	6	16	78
	ST (51)	49	51	37	63	10	90	8	16	76
	OBC (43)	30	70	19	81	38	62	15	38	47
	Muslim (13)	38	62	23	77	66	44	40	40	20
Education	High (126)	26	74	26	74	55	45	15	45	40
	Medium (125)	20	80	19	81	50	50	16	40	44
	Low (90)	37	63	24	76	14	86	3	11	85
	Nil (95)	45	55	38	62	14	86	7	12	81
Land	High (60)	27	73	23	77	44	56	5	21	74
	Medium (58)	41	59	31	69	67	33	12	38	50
	Low(109)	39	61	34	66	14	86	12	26	62
	Nil (209)	25	75	22	78	32	68	9	20	71
Occupation	Labour (186)	33	67	29	71	17	83	4	16	80
	Cultivator (93)	30	70	25	75	30	70	7	11	82
	Business (57)	28	72	21	79	42	58	13	31	56
	Service (53)	28	72	28	72	80	20	12	44	44
	Unemployed (47)	30	70	23	77	45	55	18	53	29

*Figures in percentage to total number of respondent in each background category.

Figures in parentheses indicate absolute number.

However, SC, ST people had not asserted themselves in the meetings in the way general caste people did. Only 22 per cent of SC and 24 per cent of ST people had ever spoken in Sansad meetings. In Sabha meetings the speaking rate for ST people nosedived, though for SC people the rate increased a bit. Conversely, the frequency of speaking for the general caste people (also Muslim) was far greater than other groups (65% for Sansad and 55% for Sabha).

It is not a revelation that there is close association of impoverishment, poverty and other backwardness with caste hierarchy. The lower the hierarchy the more distressing is the socio-economic conditions. At the same time, most public welfare programmes have their pre-ordained caste components, a fixed share for SC and ST people and this is the factor that not only pulls the eligible members but also pushes out those sections that are ineligible for the benefits. Such negative caste bias is one determining factor that plays a decisive part in determining the socio-economic profile of the participants. Given the pervasive poverty and predetermined scheme share for them, SC and ST people attend GS meetings in far greater number than any other categories and West Bengal is no exception to this all-India pattern. Villagers from lower social strata constitute overwhelming majority of the participants more because of the specified share for them in the welfare and other poverty alleviation schemes and their desperate necessity of assistance, and less because of the supposed generosity or pro-poor leaning of the panchayat leadership.

Education

In the sample total 126 (29%) respondents have the higher level of educational attainment, that is schooling above class X, 125 (29%) having schooling between class V-X, 90 (20%) low education implying instruction below class V and no formal education is marked for 95 (22%). The overall educational profile of the respondents is not encouraging as more than 40 per cent have either no formal education or just a shade of it. A high proportion of illiterate persons—mainly concentrated in the tribal and Muslim people of Paschim Midnapur and

Murshidabad districts—testifies two points simultaneously: the ineffectiveness or failure of the continuing (adult) education programme of the state government and the case/community dimension of the educational backwardness.

The trends observed in respect of caste are replicated in the case of education. In both Sansad and Sabha meetings the illiterate and lowly educated members participated more than any other single category (Table 3.7). In fact, illiterate members outscored every other category. Surprisingly, the respondents having middle level of education participated less than those having high or low level of education.

When the incident of speaking in Sansad is looked into, the influence of education manifests more vividly. It is the people having higher educational attainment, followed by middle level who had dominated the public speaking. Despite wide differences with other categories, the illiterate and lowly educated members were not entirely silent in those meeting though.

Landholding

Landholding, together with occupation is one important indicator of the economic conditions of the individual and family, thus a pet parameter for class analysis. However, the information about holdings is hardly authentic or reliable as villagers try to conceal, for reasons of their own, the exact quantity. An analysis based on landholding is also problematic because the nature and condition of land is widely divergent—the fertility of land and facilities like irrigation, fertiliser and use of high yielding seeds determine the produce.

In the sample total, 209 (48%) respondents do not have any quantum of land for productive purpose, 109 (25%) possess low holding size ranging between 1–3 Bigha, 58 (13%) have 3–6 Bigha placing them in the middle category and 60 (14%) hold more than 6 Bigha, thus a relatively higher scale. All information here pertains to the family holdings and not to individual ownership.

Participation in Sansad and Sabha meetings is found least among the high landholding category and higher among medium and low holding groups (Table 3.7). Those having no agricultural land also participated in those meetings. The reluctance of the big land owners was perhaps due to the very nature and character of such meetings. However, in the sphere of speaking in Sabha meetings, the ascendancy of high landholding group was evident. Seen overall, the members having intermediary holding size is found to have dominated the speaking, even though the landless people—consisting mainly of service holders—also raised their voice considerably.

Occupation

In the sample total 186 (43%) respondents are either agricultural or daily labourers, 93 (21%) are engaged in cultivation (or owner-cultivators), 57 (13%) are businessmen, 53 (12%)have service occupation and 47 (11%)are unemployed in the sense that they are not gainfully employed. Though many respondents had been engaged in more than one occupation—cultivators having business or vice versa, service holders owning agricultural land and thus income from other sources—only the reported principal occupation has been taken into consideration. Moreover, most housewives did not have personal occupation in conventional (thus skewed) sense and they are clubbed here in the unemployed category. Though many women, mainly ST and SC, were actively engaged in productive and wage employment, the casual and flexible nature of works is one obstacle coming in the way of placing them in any specified occupational category.

Whereas the labourers participated in Sansad and Sabha meetings more in number, the cultivators, businessmen and unemployed members did not lag behind in percentage terms (Table 3.7). Importantly, service holders had strong participation, accounting for a considerable presence of landless people as noted previously. In the sphere of formal participation, no distinct bias to any specific occupational group is discernable in percentage terms. At least in this respect occupation seems one neutral variable, suggesting either an equal preference by all occupational groups or influence of external inducement drawing them to those fora.

However, a different scenario is obtained in regard to speaking in those meetings. Service holders had clearly dominated the speaking—66 per cent in Sansad and as high as 80 per cent in the Sabha. The passivity of the labourers and cultivators was starkly visible. The unemployed members including some women were also vocal in those meetings.

The dominance of the service men—vast majority being primary school teachers and state government employees—in the public speaking is not surprising or this is not an aberration. It is mainly because of their involvement in trade union activities, membership of frontal organisation of parties, their exposure to mass media and peer groups, for which they can form views on developmental and community issues and can learn the tricks of public speaking. They also tend to enjoy elevated social status in the rural setting and receive favour, if not pampering, from the political parties for their pivotal role in mobilisation of the general villagers.

Party Affiliation

No serious investigation on panchayat in West Bengal can overlook the party variable for many important reasons. CPM led LFG has conceived panchayats in political terms and has placed them in a politico-administrative perspective. The party-based elections have impacted major departure from the past practices and infused many unique characteristics, especially the advent of party sponsored candidates that has reinforced party control over the functioning of panchayats and has impelled the party to be the driving force. Rural society has consequently been polarised in terms of party affiliation; politicisation has been extensive and the usurpation of even the social space by the parties has eventually transformed the villagers' live substantially and fundamentally.

The Left Front has had substantial control over majority of PRIs. During 1978–2007, the Left parties won, on an average, 65 per cent of total GP seats, 73 per cent of PS seats and 86 per cent of ZP seats. Among the left parties, however, CPM alone did have commanding position: controlling 58 per cent of GP seats, 66 per cent of PS seats and 77 per cent of ZP seats. When in 2008 elections the seat shares of the left parties decreased considerably, CPM still retained control over 46 per cent of GP seats, 49 per cent of PS and 61 per cent of ZP seats. The extent of influence of the opposition parties was only sparse and sporadic: the higher the panchayat tier the more minuscule is their presence (Appendix 1).

One important reason explaining the hiatus is the widespread network of party organisations of the Left parties, particularly CPM, their constant attempt to politically mobilise villagers as through holding formal and informal gatherings and their virtual permeation in every sphere of village life. Whether the rightist parties (Congress and TMC, etc.) are of and for the landlord and bourgeois is debatable, but one point is unequivocal. Rightist parties are based on the charismatic leadership of a few persons, their emphasis on party organisation and mobilisation of people is nearly absent and the lack of ideological and programme framework is phenomenal. In contrast to a comprehensive, well-oiled, hierarchical and cadre based Left parties, the rightist parties are based and sustained by the effort and influence of a few individual leaders.

In this context one eventuality might have been that the participation of the Left party supporters in Sansad and Sabha meetings is robust compared to the supporters of the rightist parties. Because of mass-base, cobweb of party units and frontal organisations and thrust on reaching out to more and more villagers, the Left parties are expected to bring in more people in those meeting. Also because of the opportunity offered in the informal village gatherings where people get information about political and developmental issues and receive training in public speaking, the Left party supporters are likely to be more proactive in the meetings.

An endeavour has been to ferret possible association between party affiliation of the respondents and their participation in Sansad and Sabha meetings. However, the effort has been encumbered by the volatile political situation during the time of fieldworks. While it is generally provoking to directly ask villagers about their political affiliation, the abrupt and radical changes sweeping the countryside during 2007–08 made the task even more trying and the information less reliable.

Table 3.8

Participation of Respondents by Party Affiliation

Participation	*Left Party Supporter*			*Rightist Party Supporter*		
	Yes	*No*	*Total*	*Yes*	*No*	*Total*
Attended Sansad meetings	78 (32)	168 (68)	246*	30 (29)	73 (71)	103
Attended Sabha meetings	67 (27)	179 (73)	246	25 (24)	78 (76)	103
Spoke in Sabha meetings	21 (32)	44 (68)	65	8 (32)	17 (68)	25
Spoke in Sansad meetings	Regularly	Rarely	Never	Regularly	Rarely	Never
	8 (10)	22 (29)	46 (61)	3 (10)	5 (17)	22 (73)
Received panchayat benefit	71 (29)	175 (71)	246	23 (22)	80 (78)	103

Left party supporters include mainly CPM and Rightist party supporters comprise TMC, Congress and BJP.

Figures in parentheses indicate rounded-off percentage.

* Political affiliation could not be ascertained for 87 respondents.

Since mid-2006 the otherwise calm and stable countryside has seen violent eruption and political clashes which are taking more aggressive and ominous turns after 2008 panchayat elections and 2009 Lok Sabha elections. It all started over the bid to acquire (fertile) land in Singur for setting up a small car factory, took an epoch making turn in Nandigram and spilled over to public distribution system and even to simple law and order problem. Surely, the flame and flare is confined to few pockets of south Bengal districts but the (adverse) effects could be felt everywhere in the state. Few common features of such 'mass movement' are: spontaneous and non-political growth, the initial ire against the administration ultimately took on to the party highhandedness and boycott and collapse of administration for months. Those 'public uprisings' indicated a galloping gap between the public administration and the public sensitivity and priority, corrosion of the ability of the political parties to perceive as well to palliate public grievances. The state response has unfortunately been bureaucratic and coercive counter measure by party cadres, which led to clashes, firing and loss of lives thereby aggravating the unrest and casting indelible scratches on PRIs in particular and state politics in general. In a sense, not the land acquisition per se, but the manner in which the acquirement was attempted is the root cause of the unrest. In the acquisition process everything was decided at the top and thrust upon the local administration. Rather than dialogue and consensus the 'path of confrontation' had been pursued, any consultation with and consent of the prospective evictors was never contemplated, and more importantly, the much touted PRIs including Sansad were in no way involved in the process—thus the rural people and their own panchayats were bypassed and subverted.

Such protest movements have shaken the fabrics of panchayat as well as state politics. The opposition parties, TMC in particular, could gain foothold in many villages where their streak was non-existent a few months earlier. Many villagers began to desert CPM, for instance, and joined the opposition flank. Somewhere the defection was almost total and the red forts turned into citadel of the opposition! Virtual rout of CPM in the election to the Managing Committee of high schools is a pointer to such hasty change of allegiance. The fluid party affiliation made the task of deciphering the difference on participation of the respondents belonging to left and right spectrum really tricky.

Without delving deep into the party dimensions of participation, it can summarily be pointed out that the participation of those respondents belonging to the Left parties (indeed CPM) was marginally more proactive and assertive—32 per cent and 27 per cent of the total Left party supporters attended Sansad and Sabha meetings while the corresponding figures for the rightist parties were 29 per cent and 24 per cent (Table 3.8). In the sphere of speaking in Sansad meetings some differences are evident. The Left party supporters remained less passive than the rightist party counterpart. The rightist party supporters had also received fewer benefits from the welfare schemes. Despite some intrinsic limitations, it can probably be contended that the Left parties were relatively serious and successful in assembling people in the village assemblies and their supporters were more equipped to speak in the public fora compared to the rightist party supporters.

Rural-Urban Dichotomy

Another assumption may be that the people living in those GPs that have closer proximity to the urban centres have lesser propensity to participate in GS meeting.[14] This may be due to two specific reasons. Urban adjacent GPs generally have ascending position in the development scale. The infrastructural conditions here are relatively improved and the further development demands may not be within the authority or capacity of village panchayat (drinking water, electricity, bundh). Because of the incapacity of GP to meet their major concerns, villagers, instead of pursuing their major demands, may be more interested in upkeep of the existing provisions. Furthermore, the villagers of those GPs are less dependent on agriculture. They have access to casual works (labouring of many kinds like sales, drivers) and urban recreational facilities. They have the scope to interact with urban people and can somewhat imbue the urban traits and values. The overall trends evident in Ward Sabhas of Municipality—largely urban counterpart of GS—are likely to be the pattern in such GPs.[15] Being more engrossed with income generating activities and somewhat self-centred and egoistic, majority of the villagers, except poorest of the poor, may be less interested in the occasional meeting of GS.

Those GPs located far-off from urban towns may, conversely, have contrasting demographic and developmental features. Here people are more dependent on agriculture and they have to live with less improved infrastructural facilities. The lack of access to recreational facilities and hard survival struggle may pull them to the pubic meetings where they can spend few hours leisurely. Due to the inferior condition of development parameters and straightjacket patterns of occupation, those villagers may be more dependent on panchayat and amenable to party control.

In the sample one-half of total GPs are adjacent to sub-divisional town areas and they are conceived as urban GPs. The remaining half is situated relatively remotely. From the methodological perspective, it should, however, be acceded that mere geographical location is one insufficient indicator for designating one GP as urban or rural. In fact no GP, despite sharp variation in occupational patterns, economic conditions and infrastructural status, can absolutely be urban or rural.

Table 3.9

Participation in Rural and Urban Gram Panchayats

Aspects of Participation	*Rural GP**			*Urban GP***		
	Yes	*No*	*Total*	*Yes*	*No*	*Total*
Heard about Sansad	189 (84)	36 (16)	225	171 (81)	40 (19)	211
Know the month of meeting	177 (79)	48 (21)	225	165 (78)	46 (22)	211
Heard about GUS	149 (66)	76 (34)	225	108 (51)	103 (49)	211
Attended Sansad meeting	78 (35)	147 (65)	225	57 (27)	154 (73)	211
Any family member attended Sansad	13 (6)	212 (94)	225	17 (8)	194 (92)	211
Attended Sabha meeting	68 (30)	157 (70)	225	47 (22)	164 (78)	211
Spoke in Sabha	23 (39)	36 (61)	59	15 (27)	41 (73)	56
Received benefits	72 (32)	153 (68)	225	44 (21)	167 (79)	211
Got works under NREGS	98 (44)	127 (56)	225	95 (45)	116 (55)	211
Would attend next Sansad	166 (74)	59 (26)	225	137 (65)	74 (35)	211
Spoke in Sansad	Regular	Rare	Never	Regular	Rare	Never
	5 (7)	15 (22)	49 (71)	8 (12)	19 (29)	39 (59)

* Rural GPs are Andaran Fulbari I, Golgram, Kshigram, Shaktipur and Tilpara.

** Urban GPs are Andaran Fulbari II, Malighati, Majigram, Dadpur Karidhya.

Figures in parentheses indicate rounded-off percentage.

The disaggregated responses in terms of location of GPs divulge few absorbing dimensions (Table 3.9). Regarding awareness about Sansad and GUS, the respondents of rural GPs were somewhat more cognisant and enlightened and this perhaps points to their interest in and importance of panchayat in their lives. They also participated in Sansad and Sabha meetings in larger number. Members of urban GPs scored over rural counterpart in matter of attendance of family members in Sansad meeting. May be because of other engagements or apathy, the family head had been unavailable and other family members attended.

Contrastingly, greater number of members of urban GPs spoke both regularly and occasionally in Sansad meetings and in this sphere the members of rural GPs lagged behind by 12 percentage points. But in case of Sabha meeting, more villagers from rural GPs spoke (39% compared to 27%). Furthermore, fewer number of urban GP members received scheme benefits and expressed their willingness to attend future Sansad meetings.

From the Table 3.9, implicit is the trend where villagers of rural GPs are more involved in the Sansad meetings, they are likely to use the forum for expressing or placing demands comparatively strongly. This may arguably be because of the fact that they do not have alternative avenues to seek redress of the individual or collective level miseries. Being placed differently, at least marginally, in the development scale, some sort of differences between urban adjacent GPs and others may be irreversible and GS like institution in remote areas will continue to attract more people.

Epilogue

By way of recapitulating the broad trends gleaning from the formal interview, informal discussion and anecdotal threads, it bears iteration that the Sansad and Sabha meetings are generally held and some people attend those meetings. However, those meetings are not always held as per the time schedule prescribed by the state panchayat act. There are evidences where Sansad meetings were held in one day for more than one ward, somewhere those were postponed. Such incidences do not convey a strong commitment to such grass-roots fora. The flexible or indulgent attitude of the state government to such deviation and deferment is surprising, particularly when there have been attempts to control and guide PRIs through amendment and promulgation of rules and regulations which give the impression that without some external control, PRIs would get derailed or would fail to perform the role competently, a pointer invoking the stigma of "guided panchayats". Some tough talking and strictures could have kept the Sansad and Sabha meeting on the right track.

The participation of women members, though low, is not entirely inconsiderable. For womenfolk one specific hurdle has been the timings of the meeting. Sansad meeting commences at about 5–6 PM. This early or late evening time seems inopportune or disincentive for the general women members. Here one dilemma creeps in. For the majority women members it is not always possible to venture out of home either skipping domestic chores or during evening or night. For most of them the expedient time is afternoon. But if the meeting is actually held during afternoon, as is the usual schedule, the extent of male participation would probably come down drastically. By finishing agricultural and other engagements, males find the evening slot more convenient when they get free time and can stay for longer period. Either way, one section is likely to face inconvenience and it may not be easy to meet both ends together.

The labourers constitute the majority of participants, as is the case elsewhere. By and large, the labourer, landless (also low landholding group), illiterate or inferiorly educated, moderately aged and SC, ST members throng those meetings.

The high participation rates of lower class and caste members may be stretched to substantiate a representative character of panchayats or to demonstrate a changing class forces in rural Bengal, but what is engrained on the other side of the coin also deserves consideration. The agricultural labourers comprise a formidable section of the working population in rural Bengal and their proportion is increasing.[16] Moreover, the functional domain of GP is another significant contributing factor. As the bulk of the welfare and poverty alleviation schemes have almost exclusive focus on lower class and caste people and as the deliberation in Sansad meetings revolves around those schemes, the labourer, SC and ST people will continue to constitute the majority. One hypothesis may be that the lower caste/class people attend village assembly meetings in far greater number because they are eligible for and have the needs of the benefits available under public welfare schemes and also because they, for their vulnerable socio-economic conditions, are less capable of ignoring or defying the party diktat.

The survey evidences affirm a depressing prospect for Sansad-like institution and vindicate that the positive expectations around Sansad and Sabha are awry, if not presumptuous. Surely, many assembly members have perceived Sansad as their own institution but such a conception stops short of a firm conviction. A casual or complying motive, rather than being determined to use Sansad for their own sake, tends to have prompted their participation. And this is not the prerequisite that can go a long way in making Sansad squarely public oriented or people centred.

Most of the time of a Sansad meeting is eaten up by lectures—otherwise known as *baktita* culture—and placement of reports and the general members hardly find adequate opportunity and time. The dais, microphone belongs to the leader-speaker and villagers are at the receiving end. More unlikely is a role reversal where villagers will be the speaker, provider of inputs, drawer of development plan and GP members the listener or the auxiliary agent acting in accordance with the public direction.

The administrative, audit reports of GP do not evoke public comment because either the contents are so technical or abridged that villagers find those difficult to comprehend or Sansad members are less concerned with the entire activities of GP. Neither are those reports submitted for approval of the house. The participants cannot indeed remark on many items like possible income of GP from scheme/grants, staff position of

GP, etc. They can, at best, demand higher allocation from available funds, speedy completion of a project or raise question about the rationale or justification of selecting one person as beneficiary.

Functionally, Sansad meetings are to deal with ward level concerns and development issues. But the contents of the lecture and reports cover the entire activities of GP across the territorial jurisdiction of GP and ward level issues and activities are not specifically dealt with. Indubitably, ward members are a part of GP and they have the right to know about the administrative activities and financial transactions of GP. Yet, Sansad members are immediately interested in what developmental programmes GP will undertake for the ward, what will be the allocation for the area and scheme quota and how GP will try to redress ward level problems. In other words, when the schemes and resource allocation are apportioned ward-wise and the relevant information and plans are furnished in easily comprehendible format, Sansad members may evince interest and involvement. In this respect, the ward level GP member can play a significant role. The Pradhan can be better responsible for coordinating the ward level plans and programmes. No doubt, such disaggregated allocation or schematic distribution will demand new procedures including record keeping and more work load for the otherwise under-staffed GP. But this, at least conceptually, is the frame for Sansad and herein the functionality of Sansad will probably rest.

Public view is sought at the fag end of the meeting and a sizeable section of participants do speak at this slot. Reflection on the background variables of the speakers reveals that public speaking is more dominated by those hailing from higher socio-economic strata—aged, educated, service holders and general caste people. The lower strata tend to have prostrating profile.

Almost uniformly lacking is any critical comment on any ongoing scheme, demand for reversal of the development priority, scrutiny of the activities and action of GP members and formulation of village development plan. Clear dearth even of an attempt to elicit inputs or to pass one broad framework for village development plan takes much of the shines of Sansad away. Indeed, not much concrete can be forthcoming when the obsession is with delivering lecture and placing reports.

Relating to the issues raised in Sansad meeting two types of verbal responses are generally found: pleading helplessness to consider those because of lack of authority, resource and capacity or promising to entertain or incorporate those in future occasion. Such oral promise may be politically prudent or psychologically satisfying but its material impact as through appropriate action is uncertain or could hardly be ascertained.

The nub of the matter is that no formal or official decision is taken in Sansad and Sabha meeting. By and large, no resolution is adopted in meetings, no minutes of meeting is written, official records of the meetings, wherever crudely compiled, is poorly maintained and follow-up action is seldom taken. The development decisions (including beneficiaries) are taken far removed from open forum and public glare. Going beyond the political rhetoric, it is almost impossible to substantiate whether and how far a particular panchayat decision has been conditioned by the public discussion in Sansad meeting.

Given the ambivalent, if not inconsequential, impact of Sansad-like public forum on the activities and decision-making process of GP, the promise of deepening democracy is yet to come through, literally. The paraphernalia, structure, body is there and rituals are observed. What is largely missing is vibrancy and soul.

Notes and References

1. Misra, Suryakanta, 2008. 'Thirty Years of Panchayat: The Road Traversed', *People's Democracy*, XXXII (2), May 25.
2. Particularly in Majigram GP of Bardhaman district two local leaders of CPM had taken active role in informing the date of meetings and in mobilising the people. They also reportedly spoke in Sansad meetings.
3. For a number of years, no information about those meetings could be furnished in government documents or could be made

available. In the published reports there are computing mistakes as well.

4. It is not clear from the study of Kumar (2006) whether the attendance rate was for Sansad or Sabha meetings.
5. One survey in Paschim Midnapur revealed a declining spree in the participation rates. Absence of quorum was marked in SC, ST and Muslim dominated wards and increasing apathy was marked among Muslim and higher caste people. Landless and marginal farmers mainly participated in meetings (Sau Sachinandan and Sengupta, B., 2004. *People's Participation in Grassroots Institutions of Decentralised Planning: Level, Patterns and Constraints—A Study in Kharagpur II Block of Paschim Midnapur District of West Bengal.* DRS Occasional Paper No. 15, Department of Economic and Rural Development, Vidyasagar University).
6. As one respondent put it: "Sansad is one important institution for village development. The villagers voice their demands, the annual action plan is discussed and approved there and on the basis of this plan development works are undertaken round the year".
7. The formal institution and position has certainly entered the village society and forms its politics. Yet, there remains a considerable spectrum of activities and issues that are not handled by formal institution and its representatives. A formal position does not necessarily exempt politicians from engaging in particularistic activities and CPM has exploited this avenue more successfully than others (Rudd, 2003: 153).
8. Evidences from a South Indian village indicate that officials take up to 66 per cent of the discussions and men take over 81 per cent of the discussions (Ban and Rao, 2009: 13).
9. In one instance Indira Awas Yojana was found written as *Indra* Awas Yojana.
10. NREGA is the first ever legislation that offers the rural poor the right to employment. The scheme intends to provide at least 100 days of guaranteed wage employment per family per annum. Technically, anyone can demand such works but the scheme aspires to cover those labouring poor who are out of work during the agricultural slack season.

11. Though CPM took active role in the UPA I government to push this legislation, the outreach of the scheme in West Bengal has been disappointing. During 2009–2010 (January), total 31,79,214 households demanded employment of which 31,48,275 families were provided work and among them only 10,622 (0.33%)could get work for 100 days. During 2008–09 only 1 per cent of total registered households could get works for 100 days and 72 per cent got works for 15 days only. Against the national average of 60 per cent, the state could complete 51 per cent of jobs it took up. Participation of the marginal and vulnerable groups was bad—37 per cent for SC, 14 per cent for ST and 32 per cent for women.
12. For details of women members' role in panchayats in West Bengal see Amal, Mandal, 2003. *Women in Panchayati Raj Institutions.* New Delhi: Kanishka.
13. Desai, A.R. (1969: 41). *Rural Sociology in India*. Bombay (Mumbai): Popular Prakashan.
14. A negative correlation between economic development and people's participation in Goa has been highlighted by Fernandes (1999: 158).
15. The lessons from Municipal Ward Sabhas in West Bengal are indicative for GS as well. The interest and extent of people's participation are found comparatively noteworthy in low income and slum dominated wards. The middle and high income group people tend to regard municipal services as their entitlement because of their tax payment and they avoid Ward Sabha meetings (Ghosh, Archana and Mitra (2006: 326). 'Functioning of Ward Council in West Bengal; A Case Study', in Sivaramkrishnan, K.C., ed. *People's Participation in Urban Governance*, New Delhi: Concept)
16. As per Census data, the proportion of agricultural labourers is increasing sharply—from 54.8 lakh (46%) in 1991 to 73.6 lakh (57%) in 2001—and the number of owner cultivator is declining—from 64 lakh (54%) to 56 lakh (43%) in the same period.

4

From Assembly to Committee

A Right Move!

Some states are setting up mechanism either at Gram Panchayat or ward level that can prepare, implement development plan, programme and oversee GP's development works: in the process institutionalising yet more participation of people, public monitoring and strengthening the voices of the villagers in the panchayat system. Gram Sabha in Kerala (at ward level) has the power to appoint, elect, or constitute ordinary or special sub-committee for implementing GS decision and development schemes. Two or more ward development committees may be set up in Goa for preparing ward development plan that is to be consolidated by GP and to be placed before GS for approval. There are provisions for six standing committees in Uttar Pradesh, one in Jharkhand and two in Madhya Pradesh.[1] Such committees are basically to look after the development works of GP, to improve quality and cost-effectiveness of programmes and to help in implementation of decisions of GS, if any.

Such an array of GS level committees goes a long way in accentuating and consolidating the institution of GS, mainly by overcoming its inherent weaknesses. Being an occasional village assembly, GS cannot function continuously and it cannot easily see whether and how its earlier resolutions and observations are being followed or complied with by GP. GS has to wait for the next plenary meeting for getting such information but even in that occasion time-constraint or non-cooperation of GP members may prove inhibiting. One institutional arrangement composed of able, alert and representative members may help in overcoming such structural constraints. The *Gram Unnayan Samity* (hereafter *only* GUS) in West Bengal is probably one extreme instance of such an effort.

Despite reinvigorating the panchayat system, LFG did not, for long, go for institutional reform, design change or functional refurbishing intended to strengthen the functional domain or to institutionalise participation of people. There had been no significant effort to progressively deepen the decentralisation or to equip the institutional structure, so as to reinforce public policy and revitalise panchayat vibrancy: instead, one older and therefore archaic panchayat act of 1973 continues to be the basic plank.

Barring few procedural aspects, no emphatic structural change was introduced in the 1973 act for about two decades. Only in 1992 the Gram Sabha was envisaged as an 'assembly of villagers' at the ward (constituency) level of Gram Panchayat. Thereafter, 1994 amendment act restructured the Gram Sabha with two separate entities—Gram Sabha for the entire territorial area of GP and Gram Sansad for every GP ward (also District Council at the Zilla Parishad). Incidentally, the first major structural overhauling has come through 2003 amendment (West Bengal Panchayat (Amendment) Act, 2003, (Act VIII of 2003) that has introduced Block Sansad, Zilla Sansad, Upa-Samitis at GP level and above all GUS, which is both comprehensive and controversial.

It could have been absorbing to ponder why LFG did not go for institutional reform for about three decades. Were the three tier structure and conventional functions enough or suffice even when the government's ideological perception was contrasting, commitment to empowerment of rural people unequivocal and where panchayats were considered as the strategic rural institution for furthering class interest? Though this is beyond the scope of the present investigation, it can snappily be mentioned that the ruling LFG (read CPM) has gradually moved away from its erstwhile policy of using panchayat as the means for achieving radical agrarian reforms to distinct gradualism, from an advocacy of class struggle to the "proxy class struggle" through arbitration of panchayats within the acceptable procedure (Lieten, 1996). A shift to efficient delivery of handed down programme resource is palpable. As panchayats are getting bogged down to routinism, their structural reform does not become contingent or necessary. Another significant factor has been the absolute domination of the Left parties in PRIs: had the situation been intensely competitive, the strategy and policy could well have been different. Virtual hegemonic position of the Left parties in PRIs tended to have made them somewhat complacent. Absorbingly, extensive reorientation of panchayat structure had been initiated soon after 6th panchayat elections, 2003 when the electoral fortune of the ruling front was perceived to be in danger!

GUS is one unparallel and unique institution in the discourse of panchayat. Its composition and assigned powers make GUS more than a standing committee or other sub-committee of GS being constituted in many other states. It has potentiality to transform the facets of local government to local governance. In the same vein, GUS, right from inception, is shrouded in so intense debate and dithering across political spectrum that no other panchayat institution in West Bengal has so far been subjected to. Not only for huge potential but also for the animated acrimony surrounding it, GUS deserves exhaustive assessment, to the extent presently possible.

This chapter reflects on few basic and at the same time controversial questions. Is GUS one innovative, emending, emboldening, entrenching and progressive intervention in the panchayat system? Does it furnish a new model of panchayat structure worth replicating in other states? Is GUS one anachronistic intervention that can upset the constitutional scheme and the operational ambit of Sansad and GP as defined statutorily? Can it and has it kick-started people-centred governance?

Composition and Functions

As per the provisions of 2003 amendment act, the details regarding composition, powers, functions, functional committees and accountability mechanism governing GUS are to be prescribed later on. Accordingly, the West Bengal Gram Panchayat Administrative Rules, 2004 have specified the length and breadth. However, one encounters problems in summarising the composition and accountability provisions because one subsequent administrative order (10 December, 2008) has substituted the earlier method of composition in such a fundamental manner that has upsetting impacts on Sansad's role in composition and control over GUS. The curious silence of 2008 and other subsequent administrative orders on many other related aspects compounds the confusion and suscitates an operational imbroglio.

GUS[2] is constituted for every ward of GP, as per earlier prescription, by an extraordinary meeting of Sansad to be convened by GP where the presence of 20 per cent of total members would form the quorum, failing of which the meeting would be adjourned, to be reconvened after seven days requiring 10 per cent quorum. The 2008 order has replaced the method by prescribing that the elected ward member of GP and the contesting candidate from the ward securing next highest vote in panchayat elections would sit together, unanimously shortlist the candidatures for GUS and submit the list containing the names to the Pradhan of GP, who would usually accept it and widely circulate the names for public information. If the two members cannot concur or if there is any objection from elsewhere, the Pradhan would try to resolve the issue. If the discord still drags on, the GUS formation will remain pending till further rules are prescribed. The change in the method of composition is not only radical having wider ramifications on many other related aspects but also raises the question whether the very method is reasonable and practicable.

GUS consists of three categories of members—all being members of Sansad concerned: (i) Elected panchayat member(s) and the candidate(s) securing second highest vote in the preceding panchayat poll will automatically and permanently remain members. (ii) There will be another set of ten members or 1 per cent of Sansad members, whichever is higher. (iii) Few seats will be filled from specified groups and this roughly resembles with the functional representation. One member each will be from serving/retired teachers and government employees residing within Sansad area. One member each will be from three separate Self-help Groups (SHG) having six months functioning experience. From the NGO/community-based organisation registered or recognised by the state government and operating in the Sansad area, one member each will be from three such organisations. As per 2004 rules, all the open category members were to be directly and openly elected by Sansad members present and voting. Now they are to be selected by the co-opted members of the first category. One-third of total GUS seats must be filled by women candidates.

The elected GP member from the ward concerned will be the Chairperson of GUS—in case of multi-member ward the member senior in age will preside.[3] GUS members will elect from among themselves one Secretary who will record the proceedings of the meetings, prepare financial and activity reports.[4] GUS will meet normally once in every month and preferably more frequently. Presence of one-third members in GUS meeting will be the mandatory minimum, even for adjourned meetings.

GUS will constitute few Functional Committees—presently for SHG, Education. Health and Livelihood—each comprise 4–5 members to be elected from among GUS members. Those committees will have the power to invite in their meetings subject experts for rendering non-binding advice. The stated objective of those committees is to assist GUS in discharging the functions and duties. The committees will have to work under the general direction and supervision of GUS.

Though the tenure of GUS as a body is coterminus with Sansad, confusion is compounding regarding the term of individual members except those ex-officio. As per 2004 rules,

Sansad had the power to consider the role performance of GUS members and it could annually renew or abrogate their membership. In case of termination of membership, the vacant seat(s) were to be filled by election in subsequent extraordinary meeting of Sansad. Now when Sansad has been stripped of every power over selection of GUS member, does it retain and can it perform the same review or rescinding role?

Powers and Functions

From the 2004 rules it transpires that GUS has been endowed with powers and functions that are wide-ranging, enormous (some weightier then GP's) and these are comparatively more down-to-earth and intimately related to the lives of villagers. GUS will, first and foremost, help and assist Sansad in preparing the five year perspective plan and annual plan in order to achieve economic development and social justice. Together with the formulation of plans, GUS will also implement and oversee plan-works. For performing such roles it will undertake various initiatives and accomplish functions some of which are as follows:

(i) GUS will, following participatory method, identify the special needs of the area including prioritisation of schemes/projects for implementation and for this purpose it will do many things like the following. Ascertain food security of villagers, examine livelihood option and natural resource utilisation, mobilise villagers for maximum utilisation of under-utilised natural, physical and human resources, assess educational situation and problems, consider health and nutritional conditions, seek to improve infrastructural condition, prevent marginalisation and discrimination against women and promote child development.

(ii) Plan, implement and monitor development activities including sports and culture.

(iii) Promote the livelihood opportunity for all adult members through proper and planned utilisation of available resources including greater access to credit.

(iv) Help GP to make an assessment of the tax and Tax Collector for realisation.
(v) Mobilise local resources for augmenting GP and Sansad fund.
(vi) Help village level functionaries to extend their outreach.
(vii) Ensure preparedness to prevent and tackle natural calamities, epidemics and diseases.
(viii) Promote and nurture neighbourhood groups, user groups of the poor for their socio-economic development.
(ix) Report on the progress and problems of various activities to Sansad and GP.
(x) Encourage participation of all members in Sansad meeting.
(xi) Link up activities of Sansad with GP.
(xii) Prepare budget for Sansad.
(xiii) Act as the information centre, data bank and human resource centre. Still more, the August 2006 amendment directs GUS to assist GP in identification of suitable works for providing wage based employment to the needy persons and to assist in execution of employment generation schemes to be taken up by GP.

Each GUS will prepare development plan which will be the basis of GP plan. For preparing budget, GUS will arrange the schemes, programmes and works under different groups considering the availability of fund from various programmes, untied fund from or through GP or resource generated from local area.

Moreover, GUS will have a separate fund—known as 'Sansad Fund'—that would consist of (i) grant and assistance from central, state government, ZP, PS and a certain proportion of fund raised by GP through tax collection, (ii) fund generated by GUS itself/Sansad and by way of donation from institutions for specific or general development activity and (iii) all necessary fund for a scheme, work or plan that GP may assign to GUS for implementation. One savings account is to be operated jointly by the Chairperson and Secretary, wherein all receipts will be deposited and payment made. GUS will act as the paymaster of GP for the payment of muster roll workers under any schematic or untied fund given by GP. GUS will maintain cashbook with relevant bills, vouchers, muster roll, pay order, etc. The Secretary will prepare monthly statement of receipt of fund and expenditure incurred and will submit it to GP, which will enter the information into its own cashbook. Furthermore, GUS will submit to Sansad meeting one half-yearly and one annual statement of receipts and payments during the period.

The National Rural Employment Guarantee Scheme, 2006 (NREGS) of West Bengal has further fructified the planning and implementation functions of GUS. Under the NREGS guidelines GUS, with the advice of Sansad, will prepare perspective and annual plan for the scheme works. GUS will prepare the plan of works proposed to be undertaken in the coming year and place the plan in annual Sansad meeting. The plan will be based on possible demands to be ascertained by GUS. With the approval of Sansad, the plans will be sent to GP and those will be the basis of GP's plan of work and ultimately the plan of the district, as Block and District plans are mere compilation of GPs' plan where higher tiers cannot change the priority of the lower tier. Thus, GUS will be the focal point and fountainhead of NREGS works.

GUS can play specific roles in implementation process of NREGS. First, it can, with the approval of the District Programme Coordinator, directly implement small project works. In that case GP will furnish to GUS the details of the work—cost, time-period, man-days—and GUS will place work related information/report to Sansad, not GP. Second, GUS will act primarily as a beneficiary committee and conduct social audit either directly or indirectly. Every implementing agency has to submit a report to GUS informing the estimated cost of the project, time-frame, list of labourer engaged, quality and quantity of work done, etc. Moreover, GUS will prepare its own report on the project work undertaken in the area and place the report to Sansad, including a copy to Block and District Coordinator.

Operational Experience

How GUS is being constituted, how it is performing the legally assigned role, what is the emerging relationship between GUS and Sansad, what lessons its working are unfolding are few questions that require evaluation and serious deliberation.

The first striking feature as borne out by the survey was that not in every GP and not in every ward GUS was constituted. In one GP of Murshidabad district, not a single GUS had been constituted before and after 2008 panchayat elections. In another GP of Murshidabad only three GUSs were formed, and that too under external pressure and inducement of fund.

Moreover, in some wards the extraordinary Sansad meeting was convened but because of political acrimony, violence and consequent adjournment of meeting, the formation of GUS was kept in abeyance. Where ultimately constituted, GUSs were formed without adhering to any state-wise timeframe, not only during 2005–06 but also after 2008 panchayat elections. Despite the directive to form GUS within August, 2008, they were yet to be established everywhere till November 2009. These are surprising, if not agonising eventualities in a state that can boast of deep-rooted panchayati raj.

Vacillation with GUS in the sample GPs is not one isolated instance. As per one government report, 88 per cent GUSs in the sample districts remained pending during 2005–06. In total eight districts of the state GUS formation was below 10 per cent and in Uttar Dinajpur and Dakshin Dinajpur districts the rate was well below 5 per cent, whereas the overall pending rate of the state was 77 per cent. The situation has reportedly improved during 2008–09 when 75 per cent GUSs were formed and 31 per cent of them could open account either in a bank or post office.

One absorbing dimension during 2005–06 in general and 2008 in particular was that GUSs were formed and promoted mainly in those GPs and wards that were under the control of CPM, though in one GP led by Trinamul Congress GUSs were formed during 2008. Congress and TMC were evidently averse to GUS. The perception that GUS has been devised by CPM for achieving 'political objectives' might have a hold upon their repugnance, but the basic cause perhaps lies elsewhere. This phenomenon is more closely associated with the contrasting party structure and style of functioning of CPM and Congress/TMC.

As is well known, Congress and TMC are less inclined to vertical network of party organisations at grassroots and are more dominated by few party leaders having a sphere of operational area over a locality. If few individual leaders dominate Congress/TMC party, otherwise touted as "party of leaders" rather than members—CPM is embedded in cobweb of strong party organisations, hierarchical command structure and party cadres. CPM strives for establishing party organisations—either formally or informally—at every conceivable level for involving and mobilising more and more people. Party organisations and collective decision-making premised on democratic centralism are more predominant in CPM than the dictates of individual leaders. As it visualised huge potential of GUS in mobilising villagers, CPM patently favoured the establishment of GUS and directives from party hierarchy also did not allow freedom or flexibility to the local level organisations. However, mere establishment of GUS by CPM did not imply successful role performance of those GUSs.

From the discussion with GP members and officials few reasons and insight relating to prevarication of GUS unfolded. Some GP members were loathsome to the concept of GUS. They expressed their personal inability as well as lack of organisational support for sustaining such a large public forum on continuous basis. Implicit in their observation was the detestation to their equivocal and inferior position within GUS, abhorrence to share decision-making power with many other people and opposition to the 'ingenious strategy' to trim their power.

It may be inferred that unless externally controlled and directed (as by party leaders), the positive role of GUS will largely hinge on the cooperation and support of the elected member of the ward concerned. In this context, it may be worthwhile to bear in mind that not every GP member is equally assertive, efficient, privy to scheme specific information including financial allocation and public spirited or receptive to democratic form of functioning.

Together with the grudging attitude of some GP members, the supineness of GP officials also played a part in the forestalling of GUS. As GP officials are to directly conduct and supervise the extraordinary Sansad meetings, the possibility of untoward incident, party clash and increasing load of paper and other works inhibited their interest. When large scale disruption and violence began to unfold across the state, such reluctance hardened further. One instance of such distaste can be fathomed when GP officials, particularly of Murshidabad and Birbhum districts, repeatedly claimed that they had been directed by the higher officials to postpone the formation of GUS during 2008–09 (which, we believe, is not factual).

Some GP officials and GP members raised questions over the rationale and justification of GUS. How it can be constituted and what purpose it can serve, they quipped. The village people willing to voluntarily and altruistically shoulder public responsibility are rarely available, they maintained. The debate and confusion concerning the utility and role of GUS reinforced the disenchantment of the general villagers. Some also contended that when the concept of Sansad itself has not taken firm roots—as only a handful people bother to come and they remain obsessed with individual centric economic demands—the expectation of a successful GUS and consequently a new village visage is like asking for the moon.

Regarding election of GUS members by Sansad through open election, two contrasting trends were discernable. Where one party was dominant Sansad meetings might have been untroubled but the participation of people was ritualistic. The party leaders prepared a panel and the attending people approved it without slightest murmur. The party juggernaut strangled the free exchange of opinion, meeting of minds, discussion or debate, etc.

Where more than one party had considerable sphere of influence, particularly after 2008 panchayat election, Sansad meetings were almost uniformly marred by disruption, clashes, violence and even loss of lives. The political parties mobilised villagers along party line and each tried to thwart other's bid to assume power. Thus, many meetings had to be adjourned. The administrative endeavour during 2008 to avert such political flare-up as by holding election meeting only during day-time and with police protection in sensitive wards could not effectively prevent rumpus and injury across districts.

Few Departures

Regarding open election of GUS members during 2008, many departures from 2005–06 patterns were noticeable. Earlier men and women members sat separately, presiding officer sought candidatures individually for each category of membership and party leaders (or GP members) submitted the names accordingly. In 2008, the sitting arrangement was spilt for each dominant party. The ground was vertically divided for each party supporters—men and women together—and activists of each party led people from the entrance to the sitting area. The separate sitting arrangement indicated clearly and in advance which party has the majority support and whose panel will get passage. Such an arrangement also exposed publicly the political affiliation of the people—driving out politically neutral people, if any. There was a tendency to treat family as a unit: when husband and wife had different allegiance and if they come together, wife was generally treated as belonging to husband's party. Whether one member belongs to this or that political camp became the bone of contention and often the starting point of trouble. Indeed, GUS formation by open meeting had transformed into one legislative election with all the attested features except outside supervision and protection.

During 2005–06, candidatures for each open category were sought by the presiding officer. This mandated procedure took lot of time, particularly when more candidates than available posts joined in the fray and when voice vote had to be taken for each category. Perhaps getting wiser by the experience, the general practice during 2008 was to submit a panel for all the posts at a time. When one party representative has placed one list, the presiding officer first verified whether the panel has candidates for all categories and it fulfils other requirements. If the panel was found technically correct, the names of the proposed candidates were read out and public support was sought straightway. All that took about 15 minutes to compete the election process, except where more than one panel was submitted. The strategy to save time for both GP members and officials had the degenerating effect of making the election only ceremonial, without considering whether the proposed candidates are actually present in the meeting, they are willing and whether there is other or better candidature.

Politics of Disruption—Ominous Portents

The extraordinary Sansad meeting for electing GUS members was convened on 29 March, 2005 for the constituency no. 25 of Andaran Fulbari I GP. This was the sole ward controlled by Congress party in a CPM dominated GP. Being determined to form GUS with their own party supporters, both CPM and Congress submitted their respective panels. In view of the apparent majority of Congress supporters, CPM leaders raised many objections, particularly the presence of non-electorate in the Congress panel. These provoked Congress party supporters and shouting and melee followed. Fortunately, all was verbal squabbling, worse could have happened as it was early evening and no police force was present. In the reconvened meeting, attended by BDO with large contingent of force and with abnormally high attendance of people (around 700), the Congress party sponsored panel received approval by voice vote.

For the constituency no. 24 of Andaran Fulbari I GP the extraordinary Sansad was scheduled on 4 November, 2008 at 1 PM. This was the ward that returned the lone CPM candidate in 2008 panchayat election. One discreet political alignment was reportedly contrived; CPM, BJP and others came together to defeat TMC candidates. When the rough head-count of participants indicated that CPM had the majority support, TMC leaders began to search for the strategy how to avert the humiliation. TMC leaders complained that their supporters were being dragged into the fence area of CPM. Also, CPM leaders raised objections to the presence of outsiders that TMC mobilised from other wards. Allegations, counter allegations were soon followed by altercation, brawling and beating. Soon it was pandemonium and running for cover. Police force was called in and the meeting had to be adjourned. Ironically, that meeting was yet to be convened till December 2009.

The disruption and adjournments are due to particular political configuration and the desperation of political parties to gain control over GUS. If CPM used the subversive strategy in the first instance, TMC resorted to the same tactics to scuttle the ascendancy of the rival outfit. During 2005, trouble or violence was sporadic because CPM had domineering hold. But the political position began to change after 2008 panchayat elections putting question mark on the prospect of peaceful conduct of Sansad meeting in majority GPs.

Sansad has many important statutory responsibilities and for performing those one prerequisite is the peaceful conduct of the meeting. If Sansad becomes a victim of political whirlwind, if the meeting turns into veritable battleground of parties, if the participants receive physical injury (greater than any single legislative election), Sansad can only lose its credibility and relevance. The unfolding portents since 2008 elections are ominous and Sansad as one village institution is at the crossroads.

One apparent side issue authenticates the ominous extent the village politics has plunged into and in which Sansad is to traverse its course. In one extraordinary Sansad meeting on 10 January 2006 in Daskhin Bhatibari GP of Jalpaiguri district, scuffle broke out between (ruling) CPM and TMC supporters in which many received injury and one woman died. While her husband stood with CPM supporters, the wife joined the side of TMC. This irked CPM supporters who then tried to bring the wife forcefully to their side and TMC supporters resisted. In the melee that followed, the middle aged wife was kicked in her lower abdomen. The catch here is that when TMC supporters requested the Pradhan of GP to lend his car for shifting the woman to hospital, he refused and the woman succumbed to the injury.

As per GP records, the attendance rate of members in extraordinary Sansad meetings was not that dismal. In contrast to people's attendance in general Sansad, the proportion of turnout was definitely on a higher side (Appendix 3). On an average, 147 people participated in those meetings. No meeting was adjourned due to lack of quorum. These are certainly notable features particularly when the general Sansad meetings achieve either just about 10 per cent attendance or get adjourned. Surely, the proportion of quorum was higher (double), thus more people were to be there but the point is that when achieving 10 per cent attendance is uniformly infrequent for the Sansad meetings throughout the state, no such problem plagued the extraordinary meeting.

The singular factor accounting for the participation of more people compared to general Sansad meeting relates to a concerted drive that political parties undertook. Perceiving GUS as yet another panchayat tier and centre of power below GP, parties embarked on propaganda and even door-to-door campaign asking their supporters to come and support party sponsored candidates. Such public mobilisation had made the attendance comparatively flabby, especially where more than one party enjoyed considerable support-base. However, it should not be misconstrued that because of political stake involved, almost all voters turned up—nowhere the attendance rate for the non-adjourned meeting was more than 36 per cent.

Besides GP records, peoples' responses were also collected through interview which divulged few patterns. Total 41per cent villagers were uninformed about GUS and 33 per cent attended the extraordinary Sansad meeting for electing GUS members. Thus, GUS lacked firm public prop up or public character. However, there is one regional dimension to the responses. Golgram GP of Paschim Midnapur stands apart, where majority (56%) villagers both knew about it and participated in the meeting. That GP did have considerable proportion of ST and SC population. Interestingly, the villagers participating in GUS election meetings belonged to either ST (43%), or SC (39%) or OBC (18%). From a comparative perspective, even when the vast majority of villagers (67%) stayed away, the participation of one-third respondents attests an improvement from the attendance rates in general Sansad meetings.

One inexplicable fact is that somewhere the total number of members of GUS was found to be less than 20—in 5 cases the number was around 15 and in one case only 13. The average number of members per GUS happened to be 18. Given the quota allotted to each category, the total members (irrespective of total number of voters in a ward) should not be below 20. In exceptional case, 3 members each from SHG and NGO may not be available in one ward, but still then the total members cannot anyway be less than 14. Moreover, one-third seats for women were not evident everywhere—somewhere it ranged in between 3–5. One does not know how such discrepancies crept in, persisted and why these were not attended to.

From the survey data relating to socio-economic background of GUS members (Table 4.1), it transpires that this was a forum for the older, educated, relatively affluent and exclusively for the party members. There was over representation of male members, general caste and primary members of parties in the sample. Majority respondents belonged to higher age-group, they had significant educational attainment and occupationally, most were involved in agriculture. Almost all members belonged to an age group of 40+, their educational accomplishment was well over class X, not an insignificant achievement for the older genre. Barring the service holders, all had some extent of landholdings whose size was not minuscule either. Around 6 Bigha holding is not meagre considering the average holding size in West Bengal. The economic profile roughly reveals that the membership was not open to the poorer or lower social rung. Though the members did not definitely hail from the higher strata, they were not poor either. All members were either primary party members or supporters. The field impression is that there is no real chance for a politically unconnected person to get GUS membership.

Where constituted, GUS meetings were generally held, though the frequency was below the legal stipulation. Around 42 per cent meetings could not be held at least once in a month. In meetings the presence of members was not discouraging—more than 10 members attended 64 per cent meetings.

However, it also came to notice that signatures of few members were appended afterwards—by sending register to them or arranging those wherever they were around. It was also discernable that teachers and government employees in particular were either reluctant or could not always come to meetings. Conversely, the women members reportedly took membership seriously. In overall context, except the Chairperson and Secretary, general members lacked a clear perception about the functions and role of GUS.

Table 4.1

Socio-political Background of GUS Members (figures in percentage)

<table>
<tr><td>Sex</td><td colspan="3">Male
92</td><td colspan="3">Female
8</td></tr>
<tr><td>Age (year)</td><td colspan="2"><30
—</td><td colspan="2"><50
62</td><td colspan="2">>50
38</td></tr>
<tr><td>Caste/Community</td><td colspan="2">General
58</td><td colspan="2">SC
25</td><td colspan="2">Muslim
17</td></tr>
<tr><td>Education</td><td colspan="2">< Primary
—</td><td colspan="2">< Class X
23</td><td colspan="2">> Class X
77</td></tr>
<tr><td>Land Holding</td><td colspan="2">No land
22</td><td colspan="2">1–6 Bigha
34</td><td colspan="2">> 6 Bigha
44</td></tr>
<tr><td>Irrigated Holding</td><td colspan="3">Yes
7</td><td colspan="3">No
93</td></tr>
<tr><td>Types of Residence</td><td colspan="2">All Kuchha Room
20</td><td colspan="2">Tin Shed + Kuchha Room
80</td><td colspan="2">All Pucca Room
—</td></tr>
<tr><td>Sanitary Latrine in Residence</td><td colspan="3">Yes
100</td><td colspan="3">No
—</td></tr>
<tr><td>Electric Connection in Residence</td><td colspan="3">Yes
50</td><td colspan="3">No
50</td></tr>
<tr><td>Occupation</td><td>Agricultural Labourer
19</td><td colspan="2">Owner-Cultivator
43</td><td colspan="2">Service
31</td><td>Housewife
7</td></tr>
<tr><td>Primary Members of Party</td><td colspan="3">Yes
92</td><td colspan="3">No
8</td></tr>
<tr><td>Type of Party</td><td colspan="3">Left Party
92</td><td colspan="3">Right Party
8</td></tr>
</table>

N = 32

No functional committee was ever constituted in any GUS.[5] Nor any amount was credited to the bank account. In a sense these are not surprising because functional committee can assume work only when GUS itself starts functioning and the account can have money only when GP transfers scheme or GUS generates resources by its own effort.

GUS members informed that their major activities included construction and repair of road, gravel covering of road, provision for drainage, electricity and drinking water, plantation of trees along village road, social forestry, pissiculture, work opportunity to the unemployed, distribution of houses under IAY and other permissible scheme-works under NREGS.

Operationally, most GUSs were only on paper, they floundered to take up even a modicum of the assigned functions.[6] Whatever a few GUS did was to hold meetings, discuss about projects and to forward the proposals to GP for inclusion in the Action Plan for NREGS. The selection of such project proposals was in fact termed as village development plan. Only in isolated instances, few (not all) members were actively involved in supervision of works being carried on by GP. Somewhere GUS selected one person—either from among its members or from the villagers—for doing measurement work for NREGS scheme works. Tersely, whatever GUS did was all about few proposals like road repair, earth work, garbage cleaning, pond digging, and how far those can be regarded as the village development plan in strict sense remains unclear. Preparation of perspective and annul plan and their submission to and consequent consideration by Sansad could not be traced. To be precise, perspective plan is a fiction for GP even. The annual plan is not more than a few area-wise project proposals that would be taken up under the major centrally sponsored schemes.

Whatever might have been the plan proposal and subsequent works, all entirely came under NREGS. It had obviously to be like that. For almost all GPs, NREG works now happen to be the live-blood and obsession. For instance, NREG works/projects alone accounted for 73 per cent of total budgetary estimates of one GP during 2007–08 (₹ 1.60 crore out of total 2.20 crore) and 56 per cent of another GP (72 lakh against 1.28 crore). GPs (and other tiers) have all along a clear fixation trail—once JRY, then SGRY and now NREGS. In fact, the annual plan that GPs are now preparing pertains to the project proposals relating to, broadly, rural connectivity, water conservancy and water harvesting, that would be taken up when approved and fund sanctioned. Ironically, in West Bengal NREG works have assumed eminence only recently. During 2006–07 the scheme could not make much headway for many reasons, thus the role of GUS was also subdued. Some momentum has gained only from 2007–08.

When asked, GUS members specified two problems they encountered while performing the envisaged functions. GUS could not implement particularly the programmes requiring land—the hurdle common to both town adjacent and remotely situated GPs. Adequate land was not easily available, nor were villagers willing to offer their land for the purpose of road construction or earth-work. Moreover, they found the task of selecting individual beneficiaries (IAY in particular) ticklish as the public demands far surpassed the quota available for the year. They also appraised that the general villagers were not amply aware about the functions and role of GUS, and they attributed the ignorance to the languishing economic conditions than to other factors.

Review and Reflection

GUS has many distinctive features. It can broaden the participatory plank, far more widely than any other that states ever attempted. Huge array of members may get in, certainly more than all other panchayat tiers put together. By this single stroke of the 2003 amendment, staggering number of general villagers can formally and actively be integrated into panchayat system. In 2003 panchayat elections, 49,140 GP members were elected from 42,111 wards, though the corresponding figures came down to 41,504 and 35,688 in 2008 elections.[7] When GUS with about 20 members is actually constituted in every ward of a GP, this would imply about 16 times more members than the total elected members of GPs and 13 times more members than the total elected members of all three tiers. At the same time, its functional expanse includes financial powers and executive functions like formulation and execution of plan for village development and NREG works.

GUS is presently in its infancy; it is traversing uncharted territory and striving for a new kind of relationship. As every new institution requires support on a sustained basis, any definite assertion particularly relating to the role performance of GUS will be premature. However, the prescribed institutional arrangement is one vital part that will largely determine whether GUS would perform its role successfully or not. It is important that GUS, like other public institutions, should be based on democratic principles, herein the involvement of and accountability to the people should be far and wide and the assignment of powers should be compatible with the subsidiary principle. Unfortunately, GUS lacks many structural imperatives which may not augur well for its future.

GUS raises many fundamental legal, procedural, operational questions. Exactly why has this de novo institution been designed, what are the underlying motives conditioning the course? Is the conferment of wide range of powers only by administrative rules acceptable, does not it raise question mark over the legality of the very amendment act of 2003? Is the manner of composition fairly representative or attuned to its functional sphere? Does not GUS tend to disrupt or dilute the constitutionally mandated structures or balance between tiers? Is the envisaged accountability mode adequate or can it work satisfactorily? And why is GUS fumbling to perform the assigned responsibility?

Composition Flawed

When the method of composition of GUS is closely looked at, it transpires that it is ill-conceived, nearly idealistic and somewhat surprising for the state having well-entrenched panchayats based on democratic principles and with fairly enviable track records.

The earlier stipulation of direct election has predictably proved painful and it has authenticated administrative insensitivity to the contours of political panchayat. It soon became obvious that the open election leads to serious law and order problem, raises the risk of physical injury to the villagers, publicly exposes villagers' political allegiance, vitiates the social fabric and entrenches political cleavages.

It appears that the mode of open election had been envisaged without taking into account the basic nature of party politics engrained in Bengal's panchayat system. West Bengal has political panchayats more in the sense that those rural bodies are run by the party and for the party. There was and will always be party politics, polarisation, pulverisation and political desperation to gain or regain control over panchayat institutions so long as they offer position, power and pelf. Given the functionaries, functions and fund, GUS has emphatic political importance and implications. On such a political context, the expectation of policy makers—who themselves introduced the very concept and have intimate knowledge of the working of the political panchayats—that the villagers would peacefully congregate, deliberate and unanimously decide on who among themselves would assume the GUS membership could not but be flighty one. The method of open election had been decreed without comprehending the eventuality otherwise obvious, and it resultantly turned into one inflicting adventure.

Considering the violent eruptions and ominous portents, the 2008 administrative order withdraws the open election system and ordains, what seems another dreamy dispensation. If the open election was a disaster, the revised policy assumption and prescription is no less utopian. One misadventure is being sought to be redeemed by another infeasible method. It appears that the effort to wriggle out of faux pas is creating a further mess.

The policy diagnosis—that fracas stems merely from a misconception about the purposes of GUS and all-party meeting at Block and district level will clear the confusion—overlooks, yet again, the basic character of the political panchayat. One does not know whether and how, about 18 GUS members can unanimously be picked up by two contesting candidates, invariably of antagonistic political parties (still more, GUS is expected to function on their consensus). Will the elected GP member give in to the politically incompatible demands of his adversary or will the defeated contestant endear stoical attitude? Even if an accord is anyway hammered, the internal bickering, acrimony, suspicion and other dynamics are likely to engulf the GUS and all these can make the development drive a casualty. Moreover, Indian political experience evinces that disparate parties cannot keep company for a while, even after having alternate power sharing agreement—JDS-BJP 'drama' in Karnataka being the recent case in point. More substantially, when the members of GUS are selected by only two contesting candidates, the very representative character and iota of legitimacy of the institution fritter away. It is unwarranted that such an undemocratic institution should have as significant powers as identification of the area problems, planning and implementation of development activities, prioritisation of schemes or managing separate fund. The selection method is antithetical, indeed debases the democratic ethos, otherwise engrained in Bengal's panchayat system.

Weak Accountability

How extensively and effectively one public institution is accountable to the citizens indicates its democratic character. How GUS as an institution having executive and financial power, has been made accountable is one important issue. The 2003 amendment only curtly contended that GUS "shall be accountable for its functions and decisions to the Gram Sansad" and left everything to the rules to be prescribed later on [u/s 16A (6)(c)]. The subsequent rules have charted out the details, though obliquely. Aggregating the scattered provisions in the administrative rules and other guidelines—and assuming that every other provision remains the same after substitution of open election by selection method introduced by 2008 rules—the broad methods and manners of accountability are as follows.

Sansad is empowered to make or 'unmake' GUS. All members (except the ex-officio category) hold office during the pleasure of Sansad members. GUS members' term depends on the annual consent and any member can be removed (and replaced?) by Sansad. Moreover, in half-yearly and annual Sansad meetings GUS will place two reports—one about the work/scheme already undertaken and another about statement of fund received and utilised. The five-year perspective and annual plan prepared by GUS will have to be approved by Sansad and only thereafter can be sent to GP for preparing GP plan. Regarding statement of funds received and expended, the Gram Panchayat Audit and Accounts Rules inform that Sansad members can ask for any information as to the receipts and payment and GUS is bound to furnish the same. Therefore, Sansad members may criticise and suggest corrective measure(s) and GUS is to comply with it, a framework consistent with legislative-executive dispensation.

The Pradhan, Sanchalak of Upa-Samity, Executive Assistant, Secretary of GP and government officials shall have the power to make inspection over GUS accounts, registers, documents and works. GUS will have to furnish to GP (i) the source, purpose and utilisation of public donation, gift received, (ii) the monthly statement of all receipts and payment together with papers and vouchers which will be entered into the cashbook of GP. Thus, GUS fund is integrated with that of GP and subjected to audit. Interestingly, while there is no organic linkage between GUS and GP—except the ward member being GUS chairperson whose powers and accountability therein are far from clear—GUS is to submit to GP the monthly statement of accounts, half-yearly and annual report. GP can delegate schemes along with fund and it will retain the control over the fund that GUS can generate by its own efforts.

By and large, GUS remains responsible to Sansad, where villagers collectively can exercise accountability. Having the most intimate proximity, such public control is expected to be fairly overwhelming. Notwithstanding the conceptual fineness, is Sansad exercising accountability or is it in the present political context really capable of? It requires emphasis that nowhere Sansad has ever commented adversely on the report of GUS or recalled any member. Role reversal can be possible where one dominant party loses strength considerably or the opposition party gains support-base—then Sansad platform may be used for criticising, discrediting or for recalling purpose.

Few fundamental aspects need consideration. What if GUS submits no report, if any discrepancy, misappropriation of fund is detected? If fund flowing from GP is not properly utilised or if supporting vouchers are not placed who will be responsible for and how can the accountability be enforced? One should be cautious in regarding Sansad as the collective forum where villagers have got the 'power to' direct their representatives. Sansad is one deliberative body, its meetings are called by GP and there is no provision for requisition meeting (unlike 1957 Act). What happens if any meeting is not called or one meeting is held for more than one Sansad areas? How can Sansad then oversee the activities of GUS?.

When the electorate is generally averse to asking questions and elected representatives strongly resist public scrutiny, can U-turn be feasible at Sansad level? The people attending Sansad meetings are supporters of the ruling party and they are merely 'onlookers' rather than active participants. The position of the general villagers aggravates when GUS members have, in general, higher status and connection with the (ruling) political party. The emerging trends testify that the legalese is to lose relevance, sooner than later. Whenever GUS is working, the resolutions, recommendations of Sansad are practically the handiwork of a handful GUS members; few politically influential members are preparing plan proposals, schemes for NREGS, etc. and Sansad is giving formal seal of approval to those. GUS tends to have institutionalised what was earlier going on informally. It is 'caucus over masses', 'power over' people rather than 'power to' them.

Marginalising Gram Panchayat

GUS has the potentiality to impact profound changes in many aspects of panchayats process, full dimensions of which are unfolding gradually. One such impact relates to the planning and programme implementation process. GP was, for long, responsible for deciding projects, finalising allocation of fund and execution of projects. Then Sansad became the planning unit—a contravention of prerogatives of GP and a recipe for procedural bottlenecks. The 1994 amendment ordained that Sansad would identify schemes on priority basis for development of the village and every Sansad resolution/ recommendation would be binding in nature. Now the situation undergoes further changes. The statutory provisions make GP's choice and action fairly constricted. GP has no option but to act upon all Sansad recommendations relating to prioritisation of the list of beneficiaries, scheme/programme (s/19(3)) and to duly consider every Sansad resolution (s/17A (3)). With the help of GUS, Sansad will now prepare perspective and annual plan, on which the plan of GP would be based. GUS will select project, implement and supervise works, select people for beneficiary oriented schemes, decide how villagers can participate in project implementation. For different kinds of works, the functional committees of GUS will take over. Tersely, GP will formally be the overall in-charge and undertake only those works that extend to more than one ward. And GUS is likely to encroach upon and usurp powers that belong to GP, constitutionally and operationally.

All these tend to stymie the powers of GP and to reduce it to only coordinating or attesting office. This may lead to a ticklish situation. When the resolutions, plans, prioritisation of Sansad are obligatory on the part of GP, problems are likely to bedevil the planning process.[8] What if one Sansad recommendation is incompatible with another, or if the development strategy of GP is contradicted by one Sansad? It is one thing to seek people's priority and entrench participatory process but completely another when Sansad is made the planning unit without fixing parameters governing the planning function and without empowering one institution to take final decision in terms of viability of the suggested projects and resource availability.

A Four-tier System

Government documents avouch that GUS is not another tier, not one parallel institution. It is rather one statutory sub-institution, one executive arm of Sansad that would work as the most powerful and intimate organisation of the villagers. It would assist and work in league with GP. However, GUS is practically another panchayat tier, virtually a micro GP at ward level. As noted already, the powers and functions of GUS extend to important gamut of development process including control over functional committees and development fund.

With the onset of GUS the panchayat system in West Bengal reverts back to the four-tier structure, roughly resembling with what the Panchayat Act, 1957 and 1963 together established. The 1957 act envisaged *Gram Sabha* for every 'gram' (present-day GP ward) consisting of all registered electorate (about 1,000–1,400) pertaining to the gram and for each gram one *Gram Panchayat* with 9–15 members to be elected by the Gram Sabha members from among themselves. Gram Panchayat was the executive agency of Gram Sabha. Members of Gram Sabha statutorily had controlling power over Gram Panchayat—it could consider, in the annual meeting, the budget for the coming year and other Gram Panchayat reports containing works done and proposed to be undertaken. Besides giving necessary suggestion, Gram Sabha did have the right to ask for any information from Gram Panchayat relating to administration (s/8 (2).

Almost similar situation is now unveiling. Sansad is like *Gram Sabha* and GUS is a replication of *Gram Panchayat* (by virtue of area, composition, functions and accountability). However, there are few differences. The 1957 act had detailed provisions relating to the composition and functions of Gram Panchayat and Gram Sabha. But GUS is practically a creation of administrative rules. Under the 1957 act the extraordinary meeting of Gram Sabha could be held upon a written requisition of not less than 1/5 of total members. For Sansad there is no such provision for requisition meeting. Sansad has a defined role and elevated status, its recommendations are final and obligatory in nature. But Gram Sabha under the 1957 act suffered from statutory ambiguities. Under the 1957 act Gram Sabha did not have the power to remove Gram Panchayat members but Sansad now theoretically enjoys such power over elected GUS members. GUS has larger number of members, one Secretary and functional committees and its members are not integrated with any other tier. Under 1957 act the Gram Panchayat members were ex-officio members of the *Anchal Panchayat*, the next higher tier for a group of gram panchayats.

The 1957 (and 1963) framework did not get a fair trial, the system died as soon as it was born. By reverting back to the erstwhile structure or ordaining a configuration that no other state has so far attempted, is West Bengal furnishing a new model or direction? Is the model a progressive one or is GUS more like a cosmetic make over, a clever move to conceal the seamy sides or divert attention from the basic maladies of the system?

GUS has prominent powers and sweeping role, it is virtually another panchayat tier. In this context one pertinent question is whether the conferment of so wide assortment of powers and functions only through the administrative rules is preferable or acceptable and is not the divestment of so significant aspects of legislation an instance of 'excessive delegation'. The situation gets murkier when it is found that the 2003 amendment itself has elaborated bolts and pieces of all other newly introduced structures like Upa-Samity (of GP), Block Sansad, Zilla Sansad, etc. It is only for GUS that the amendment act offers one blueprint and that too only rough and short.

Why the Samity?

More substantial and at the same time polemic question is why such an important structural intervention has been envisaged and that too in a hurried way without even taking other 'junior' LF partners into confidence and disparaging all trepidations and opposition. What are the specific purposes the institution intends to serve? The canvas gets confounded when the intervention evokes both adulatory reception and apprehension and the avowed objective of GUS is short and old.

The apprehension and scepticism about GUS basically veer around the motive and consequences of the structure so enjoined. The way in which the amendment act, 2003 containing the provision for GUS was rushed through provoked demurring. Some suspected that the political landscape during and after 2003 panchayat elections impelled CPM to plan for GUS-like institution mainly as a political design or cushion. The 2003 election was the bloodiest—with 80 death tolls during and after poll. In that election the proportion of uncontested panchayat seats was so far highest.[9] Some went on to claim that unusually higher proportion of uncontested seats was the outcome of widespread intimidation and subjugation that was resorted to sail over the unnerving prospect of losing panchayat power. The use of threat and violence reported in media also created an adverse public reaction, to some extent at least. At the same time, the opposition parties gained control over panchayats in higher proportion than the previous occasion—Congress party won two ZPs, for instance. In this context it was perhaps politically prudent to plan one institutional arrangement that could explicitly be pro-people but implicitly and simultaneously could serve few political purposes such as: (i) to help accommodating those who have lost seat in panchayat election. The lucre of power and pelf available with GUS would possibly prevent their migration to 'greener pasture'.[10] (ii) GUS would institutionalise the so long informal 'reign' of local level party leaders who had been controlling the panchayat decision-making since long. (iii) And GUS would help in circumventing the hold of the elected members of a GP, in case non-left parties win power. Incidentally, except CPM, all left and right parties publicly vented their concern and opposition.

Many feared that GUS is one clever move for supplanting the elected GP. It had been dubbed as a "sinister move" to gain total 'Marxists control' over panchayats, for usurping the role of Sansad by party leaders through the backdoor and a "façade for a hidden agenda".[11] Some also resented the unbridled powers for this contrived mechanism.[12] Some apprehended that GUS would create new rural oligarchy and start a new rural power game. Few non-political organisations like Rajiv Gandhi Foundation regarded it as one undemocratic and retrograding attempt that would shake and debase the very foundation of panchayat.

One assertion is that GUS is one adapted and distorted version of the Convergent Community Action (CCA) that emerged out of the experiment of *Gram Unnayan Kendra* at the behest of the IIT, Kharagpur and Midnapur ZP where it was vindicated that the village level planning by villagers themselves is indeed possible. The argument is that GUS is a new avatar of old CCA, with a newer accent on mobilisation and utilisation of local resources.[13] However, it may be pointed out that given the solid structure and comprehensive functions, GUS is different from CCA or it is something more than simple village planning by villagers.

Many have thrown weight behind it and regard GUS as a welcome extension of the lower tier for effectuating greater transparency and accountability in development activities, a 'bold step' to substitute representative *raj* by open and direct participatory democracy. GUS is the right move away from bureaucracy-led district administration and bureaucratic GP to a people centred governance. GUS is expected to ensure that individuals and social groups get benefits from various development programmes and force GP to devise pro-people and community centred plans and implement those more effectively than ever. Being the lowest and smallest unit of the development process, GUS can identify the cause and suggest the appropriate remedy with microscopic precision for local level problems. Moreover, as the majority members come from non-political background and with proven social commitment, political division or wrangling would not vitiate the functioning of the Samity and it would be able to strive for local development more intimately and effectively.

The CPM spokespersons clarified that GUS in particular and the 2003 amendment in general was an earnest attempt to put into practice what was declared in the Election Manifesto of the Left Front—to make panchayats more people oriented and effective. The fervent claim is that GUS would offer to the general villagers the opportunity to directly participate and direct rural development process, it would reduce incidence of power concentration in few hands. By empowering general villagers, GUS would ensure that development plans are formulated according to the perception and priority of the villagers, peoples' involvement in implementation would minimise the possibility of delay, corruption, etc. As to the question whether GUS was a ploy to control opposition party led panchayats, the quip was that as the Left Front control vast majority of GPs, GUS would instead give more participatory space to the opposition parties.[14]

For few years CPM was insisting on reforming panchayat system on two counts: to inject more participatory character and to overcome concentration of power at the hands of the Pradhan of GP. However, the veracity of the insistence on outdoing power concentration at Pradhan's hands is to be accepted with a pinch of salt. The Pradhan in a CPM controlled GP cannot unilaterally do much. Together with directives coming regularly from party hierarchy, there is one informal committee—*Pradhan Sahayak Committee* that, consisting of important village level party leaders, takes all important decisions, which Pradhan formally endorses and implements. At the same time, the *Upa-Samities* as envisaged by the 2003 amendment affectively clip the wings of the Pradhan. Thus, further curtailment of power would reduce him into just one figurehead. It also needs emphasis that GUS practically trims down powers of GP members individually and of GP collectively and not specifically of the Pradhan. Moreover, if power is being concentrated in the hands of the Pradhan of GP, what about the Chairpersons of other tiers?

The statutory objective of GUS is to ensure "active participation of people in the implementation, maintenance and equitable distribution of benefits" [s/16A (c) (1)]. In fact, participation and involvement of people in the development process has now become a fad, a new mantra—almost everyone and everything avouches the objective. Noteworthy is the fact that the same objective was earlier served for a decade by the Beneficiary Committee. The 1994 amendment act envisaged Beneficiary Committees to be constituted by GP with the advice of Sansad for performing hosts of functions. However, the working of Beneficiary Committees was hardly satisfactory: not constituted everywhere, manipulated by the ruling party and both villagers and GP members having a blurred conception of it (Bhattacharya, M., 2002: 136). Objective-wise, both Beneficiary Committee and GUS belong to the same genre. It remains blurred what specific factors have prompted the substitution of Beneficiary Committee by GUS, thus some conjecture or reading between the lines may linger on.

Motives are things notoriously difficult to pinpoint, more so in the Indian political spheres. Yet, one thing is almost incontestable: PRIs do operate in a political ambience. The party in the state power uses PRIs in such a way that offers maximum possible political mileage to it. However, the moot question is whether the political calculations or considerations should always prevail over the developmental imperatives and whether the 'party political objectives' will be allowed to make panchayat a casualty.

A Compendium

The extensive powers make GUS one inimitable as well as formidable grassroots institution. The effort to integrate whooping number of general villagers in the development and implementation processes is commendable. This intervention attempts to entrench participatory development and offer more power to the people, rather than to a handful of elected representatives. GUS can minimise the possibility of power concentration in few hands and uphold the notion of 'localised development'. Acting as the executive arm, GUS can reinforce the role of Sansad and impart people's perspective into GP activities. However, eyebrows regarding its composition and weak accountability cannot be brushed aside.

Discernable is idyllic romanticism in the method of composition and the inertia of the administration towards fructification of GUS. The latest method of composition by consensus between two candidates belonging to warring parties seems not only undemocratic but also least pragmatic in the political panchayats. Under the erstwhile method of open election by Sansad, GUS might not have been formed with enough public support, but that procedure was relatively democratic and less detestable. Whatever modicum of democratic element was evident earlier has now been effaced where villagers do not have any voice whatsoever. From democratic standpoint, any institution composed of members selected by only two persons ought not to have such significant and encompassing powers.

GUS perhaps typifies an overdrive of democratisation and testifies an initiative taken hastily without considering or grasping possible legal, administrative and political intricacies and fallouts.[15] The apprehension raised at the outset that GUS would lead to overlapping of functions and would usurp the power of GP has somewhat been vindicated by the administrative rules, 2004. Sansad, one deliberative body, may have got its executive arm but the new dispensation is likely to rob the role of Sansad in practical, if not in the legal sense—GUS is likely to assume supremacy over Sansad, just in the same way the parliamentary form of government is evolving. GUS has the potential to become a monster, literally. Because of pervasive political control, party politics, and its few inherent weaknesses, Sansad is unlikely to outmanoeuvre the overdrive of GUS, if any. This is why some regard GUS as a retrograde step, one unnecessary, inconvenient, unwieldy and arguably unworkable structure.

From the operational standpoint, some disquieting dimensions come out in the open. GUS had not been constituted everywhere—either for repeated adjournment of Sansad meetings or for administrative negligence. Administrative initiative towards forcing compliance to the statutory provisions did not follow in many instances. In majority cases GUS was hardly functioning. Such non-starter nature—attesting either a lackadaisical approach or a wait and watch strategy—has unwittingly become a blessing in disguise because many procedural, practical and political problems could otherwise have constrained GP process. Even in the face of 'ceremonial' role, the value of GUS as one mobilisation plank was evident and after panchayat elections the village politics revolved around GUS. Political parties perceived GUS as yet another centre of power and an additional fount of rural power base. And this is basically the reason for which there had been and will arguably be intense political wrangling and clashes among political parties, for which GUS will probably find it tricky to perform its role successfully.

Besides debasing the constitutional scheme, upsetting the decentralised planning process and politically polluting the rural society, the objective of GUS tends to be rhetorical and obscure. At present, the functional efficacy of GUS is unimposing and this gives short shrift to the high hopes surrounding it. Furthermore, the 'pious' expectation that the members in general and Secretary of GUS in particular, would shun self-interest, political affiliation and would work collectively with a commitment to the commons may be fine in print but the gut issue is whether such a genre is actually left over and if at all, will it be allowed to function in an insulated or unencumbered way.

Notes and References

1. Instead of 8 sub-committees prescribed by 2001 amendment, there are now two such committees in Madhya Pradesh, namely *Gram Nirman Samity* and *Gram Bikas Samity.* There are Monitoring and Vigilance Committees in other states.
2. Gram Unnayan Samity is different from *Gram Unnayan Committee* which has been formed by villagers of Paschim Midnapur district reportedly to counter the alleged highhandedness and arrogance of CPM leaders.
3. In case of resignation, leave of absence or death of Chairperson, the Pradhan of GP will preside over.
4. The selection of Secretary has proved problematic. The general perception is that it is one government post and the Secretary holds the purse of GUS. However, this is one honorary position

and some financial assistance may be granted out of 'Sansad Fund' for specific activities if Sansad and GUS approve it. The Secretary is expected to be a man of integrity, honesty, public spirited, enjoying people's trust and having sufficient time for public works.

5. One Sub-Committee on Village Health and Sanitation has been formed, not specifically under 2004 rules but as per requirement and guidelines of National Rural Health Mission (NRHM) in GUSs of 8 districts during 2008–09. Such committees consisting of at least 50 per cent women are responsible for planning, supervising and implementing activities relating to maternal and child health. NRHM fund @ ₹ 10,000 has been allocated to the Sub-Committees and weight machines have been purchased (GoWB, 2008: 50).
6. However, to one estimate, initiatives of GUS secured community contribution to the tune of 10–40 per cent of total Sansad plan budget, created valuable assets through implementation of planned activities and increased participation of people in Sabha and Sansad meetings, both qualitatively and quantitatively. Many GUSs collected socio-economic information through neighbourhood meetings, developed baseline for planning purpose, identified out-of-school children, mother and children remaining out of enteration, launched campaign against social evils and helped forming of women SHGs (GoWB, 2006: 116).
7. Now, after reorganisation of panchayat constituencies, there will be one GP representative for every 900 electorate (instead of 700). As a result, the number of GP constituencies has come down by 18 per cent (from 42,111 in 2003 to 35,688 in 2008) and total number of GP members decreased from 49,140 to 41,504. The purported purpose, that is to offset the steep rise in the number of electorate, remains contested when there is 6 per cent increase in ZP and PS seats.
8. Ghosh, Buddadeb, 2003. 'Much Ado About Nothing; West Bengal's Panchayat Reform', *Panchayati Raj Update*, August 7.
9. The total number of uncontested seats was abnormally high: 11 per cent in GP, 10.3 per cent in PS and 4.5 per cent in ZP. This is surprising particularly for GP where the average number of

contesting candidates is 3 and where the margin of winning and defeat is about 10–30 votes.

10. Bandyopadhyay, D., 2003. 'The Caucus and the Masses', *Economic & Political Weekly*. November 15, 4825–27. Also 'Panchayat Puzzle', *The Statesman*, August, 11–12.
11. *The Statesman* (Editorial), August, 11, 2003.
12. "We have been emphasising that the formation of any other committee in addition to the existing panchayats is harmful for democracy. We have repeatedly said in Left Front meetings that there is no need of any nominated committee when there is an elected panchayat for rural government". RSP Secretary Mr Bandopadhyaya, quoted in Chakroborty, Asish, 2003. 'New Fount of CPM Rural Power'. *The Telegraph,* July 11. Another RSP leader moaned: "we saw the game for what it (GUS) is but were forced to fall in line."
13. Chatterjee, Arnab, 2003. 'Old Wine, New Bottle, Panchayat Planning in West Bengal'. *Economic & Political Weekly*. 38 (38).
14. Anil Biswas, former Chairman of the Left Front, at the press conference on 10 July, 2003, as reported in vernacular press.
15. Incidentally, it has been argued that a clearly thought out policy in advance of implementation was not the habit of LF government. In many instances the government had to backtrack (Mallick ,1993: 168).

5

Travesty of People's Raj

Gram Sabha is one unique institution in many ways. Structurally, it is akin to one assembly of electorate having the authority to exercise accountability over the elected Gram Panchayat members. It has the potential to reshape the character and redress the otherwise deficient democratic governance in rural India. Operationally, it tends to be one groping institution where the failings surpass the success. Utility-wise, GS serves the interests more of the politicians and less of the villagers for whom the assembly is primarily intended.

To give fillip to and to reorient the vibrancy of GS, two separate years have already been celebrated as the Year of Gram Sabha. But such celebration has admittedly been on a rather disquieting backdrop. "Although the Gram Sabha forum has high potential for grounding democracy at the grassroots, facilitating socio-economic inclusion, participation in planning and implementation of development programmes and ensuring accountability of the Panchayat to the electors, it is generally seen that meetings of the Gram Sabhas are not held regularly and are marked by thin attendance particularly of women and marginalized groups. There is little discussion on the proposals put forward for approval by the Panchayat. Issues of common interest and of the marginalised sections are often not discussed .... The task before the Gram Sabha is approval of the lists of beneficiaries, approval for issue of utilization certificates and passing of the annual accounts. Panchayat heads bring their own supporters and potential beneficiaries to attend the meetings .... Hence, a sense of cynicism has developed about the efficacy of Gram Sabha meetings .... State Governments have been rather slow in investing the Gram Sabhas with the requisite powers."[1]

To many commentators, GS must succeed because it has far-reaching multidimensional underpinnings and potentialities. It is supposed to be the most intimate representative decision-making institute which can realise the ideals of democracy. When government is of the people, development is by the people and for the people, GS would set the agenda, oversee the expenditure of tax payers' money, stop wastage or irregularities in implementation process, seek clarification, express public grievances, evolve mechanism and conduct social audit, enhance efficiency, transparency and responsiveness in the functioning of local governments and all these with least expense and fairly easily. Though GS is presently not performing its role successfully, the fumbling is said to be momentary and everything can and should be set right through careful nurturing with focussed approaches and appropriate strategy. Being the fulcrum of the entire decentralisation scheme and the bedrock of democratic governance, GS ought to be made a powerful and pulsating village institution. In hindsight, it appears that such normative basis and the tendency to proceed from conclusion to premise is inflicting indignity to GS.

For deepening and strengthening decentralisation process, wider and active participation of people is sine qua non. People's representatives may have been elected but they cannot substitute the people. In recent discourse on democracy, participation of people in the political decision-making is valued because it would strengthen the accountability of the democratic institution, as by increasing the intensity and ties between people and representatives, by exposing and subjecting the institution to the continuous community scrutiny and by forcing the institution to be responsive to the popular priorities. The inputs and pressures from the people will provide need-based information and demands to the decision-making centre, thus making direct impact on the developmental benefits, more so when the traditionally marginalised sections assert their preferences. Yet, such theoretical premise is hardly corroborated by the working and outcome of the envisaged instrumentality, almost in every country.

Conceptually, GS is intended to empower, enlighten and engage the rural people in the process of local governance. Operationally, its role is hardly satisfactory and GSs in most states are said to be somewhere in the twilight area between the rule of the few and rule of the masses (Fernandes, 1999: 180). The gut issue, thus, is what are the constraints and handicaps that hold its role performance or impose barriers to its elevation to one primary village institution. The studies investigating the working of GS have identified three broad types of constrictions.

The negative responses and reluctance of GP members contribute to the ineffectiveness of GS. Many GP members are hesitant to face the electorate, wary of public control or impervious to critical comments and they try to scuttle the prospect of people's participation and popular control. Questions from the villagers irritate, if not outrage them, they feel uncomfortable in going to people with their cards open. They follow few strategies like deferment, postponement of meeting under trivial pretext, arrange meeting on a day when majority of villagers would face inconvenience, hold back information of meeting, invite their supporters or cronies and refrain from propagating the importance of GS and right of the villagers. GP members furnish, though subtly, few arguments in defence. GP is overburdened and incapable of maintaining procedural and additional paper works relating to the meetings. Constructive discussion and collective interests are barely in display in such meetings. Instead, the opposition groups or party supporters try to malign or discredit the ruling members or try to settle personal scores. And GP does not have the resource base and administrative capacity to consider or fulfil the demands of the villagers.

The general villagers have blurred conception about the powers, authority of GS and they are oriented to perceive GS as one government institution for undertaking development works and distributing scheme benefits. They hardly evince interest because such meetings seldom have tangible or positive outcome. The opportunity cost of participation is not commensurate with the possible gains. Whenever some people express views, submit plan proposals these are not usually accepted or acted upon. Such negative impression is one reason why participation rates slump in subsequent meetings. The obsession with selection of beneficiaries and absence of emphasis on overall village issues drive the affluent sections away. Women members have very nominal presence in those meetings because of variety of reasons: patriarchal values, social subjugation, inconvenient time of meeting, occasional violence and lack of education and information.

GS stumbles to emerge as one reverberating institution of participatory democracy as the very institution has been thrust upon from the above. Everything has been decided by the governments and villagers are expected to endear the concept, activate the forum and actualise the potential. If the communitarian panchayats and informal village assemblies were autonomous, consensus making flexible institutions, the present form of GS is absolutely formal, institutional and political. Any institution conceived and created by a top-down dispensation cannot obviate socio-political dynamics. In every village both divisive and integrating forces are at work and the newly introduced structure often exacerbates the divisive forces.

Few other inconsistencies also merit mention. GS meeting, agenda items, thread of discussion and follow-up action all depend on the cooperation and support of GP members, particularly the chairpersons. In case GS meeting is postponed, if adopted resolution is not complied, GS members can do little, and more importantly, they have not gone to enforce whatever rights they presently have. Ironically, the directors, so to say, are sought to be directed by the dependents.

From the perspective of its composition, GS is encumbered to express itself and somewhat disqualified to act as the deliberative and collective decision-making body. It is difficult to ascertain or enlist the views of the participants or hammer out consensus in an open and large gathering. Voting on a particular issue may lead to disintegration or may accelerate socio-political divisions among villagers. Following Athenian suit, the demagogues or influential party leaders may sway the public opinion. When decision-making is one long dilatory process, when it is difficult to saturate the aspirations of many, GP members may not entirely be faulted if they are inclined to take decisions outside of GS forum.

Mere assemblage of some people means little. A pragmatic approach and sound planning is absolutely essential. Here the Kerala instance is illustrative. Even the meticulous strategy of the People's Campaign that followed massive propaganda, groupings of participants on single development issue and passing the group recommendations at the plenary session of meeting could not realise many of the supposed potentialities of GS. On this backdrop, how can unstructured and unplanned village assembly meetings, as is the case in most states, be invariably effective and productive?

Even in the polished and protected legislatures, unruly behaviour, free-for-all showdown, abusive and unparliamentary practices are not uncommon. In a remote rural setting how far is it feasible to ward off political rivalry, personal animosity and clashes over the share of public gift or garnering political position (like GUS membership)? If, for instance, majority participants try to confront the decision of GP or if anyone goes overboard, who is there and how to prevent the disruption? The participants have heterogeneous background, they clamour for public benefits, they are disorganised and all these make it difficult for GS to evolve as one coherent and practicable working forum.

What is absorbing is that the conventional constraints like multi-layered, heterogeneous and hierarchical social relations, unequal power structure and lack of functional autonomy as well as political will would not hold much water in West Bengal if the (political) claim of LFG—that an objective condition for the culmination of local democracy has been set in rural West Bengal—is to be believed. Nonetheless, the ground reality, as the survey results unfolded, is not fundamentally different from rather dismal records obtained in other Indian states. GS meetings are not always held, indeed all the meetings following the prescription of the state panchayat act have never been held in any single year. Even when such meetings are actually convened, the participation of villagers, more so of women, leaves much to be desired. The view, preference and priorities of the villagers do not usually get reflected in the decisions, plans and action of the GP concerned. Sansad and Sabha are yet to emerge as one effective and powerful collective decision-making platform. People's participation is more or less ritualistic as far as the outcome of the meeting is concerned. The selection of scheme beneficiaries through open forum is almost a myth. Worse still, the powers of Sansad are getting confined to only approval functions (see section below). The popular voice is being controlled, if not chocked. GP members (and party leaders) dictate and decide and people remain listeners and spectators. The fine-tuning of Sansad by providing one executive arm in the form of GUS seems preposterous and retrograding because it has already exacerbated the political divisions among villagers and marred the functionalities of Sansad. If and when GUS starts functioning in real sense, it can hijack the role and authority of Sansad.

What then would explain the yawing chasm between the positive claims and functional inadequacies of Sansad and Sabha in West Bengal? Seen overall, it would be naïve to evaluate or treat the functioning and efficacy of Sansad and Sabha in isolation and it should better be posited on the wider perspective of the functional domain of PRIs, especially GP and the political process conditioning the operational ambit of PRIs. The role of Sansad and Sabha is inextricably associated with the functional spheres of GP: in fact, these village institutions seek to insert popular approval, advice or control over what GP does. The programmes and activities being undertaken by GPs will supply the substance and meaning to the interest and involvement of villagers. If and when GPs have statutory powers and resources for addressing community issues and problems over which villagers have direct and collective stakes, the people can be enthused and involved. At the same time, how the panchayat decisions are being taken is equally important for the successful evolution of Sansad-like institution. Notwithstanding the nature of GP's powers, if the decision-making process is held hostage by a coterie and if public participation and inputs are discounted, the prospect of participatory democracy will remain elusive.

Functional Domain of GP

Since inception of statutory panchayats, one central question has been whether PRIs are for development purpose or for the wider intent of self-government. Unfortunately, PRIs are locked primarily for development purpose and that too on the basis of conditions imposed and resources devolved from above. The plain fact is that PRIs are engrossed with implementing public schemes and programmes. Neither they have strong resource base nor do they tap possible sources of revenue.

Funds firstly from the state government and thereafter from centrally devised development programmes have been keeping PRIs in West Bengal going. For instance, during 2005–06 the per capita own source of revenue of GP—upon which the capacity to function as self-governing unit depends heavily—was just ₹ 8.7,[2] and this amount was used not for productive but for contingency purpose (GoWB, 2008: 108). At the same time, GPs hardly have authority over majority of schemes and programmes being implemented at village level.[3] While the line departments of the state government handle most of the schemes, the sphere of GP is categorically confined to few centrally sponsored 'tied' ones. The operational domain of GP offers little credence to the claim that most of the functions listed in the 11th schedule of the Indian Constitution have been devolved to PRIs in West Bengal (also elsewhere). The consequent external subvention forces GP (and other tiers) to be mere implementing agency, stifles its capacity to assess and respond to local area needs and thwarts the possible demands for functional and financial devolution for providing better services to the local people.

The budgetary allocation of the sample GPs reaffirm that centrally sponsored schemes are the livewire for them. Out of total allocation during 2007–2008, the source of funds and allocated expenditure on an average were as follows: (i) 0.9 per cent fund coming from own source of revenue was allotted for the purpose of education, health, infrastructure, women and child development, agriculture and animal husbandry. (ii) 7 per cent fund received as grants-in-aid was for remuneration, recreation and incentive purpose. (iii) 15 per cent coming from state government, MLA local area development scheme was intended for infrastructural improvement and continuing education. (iv) 67 per cent fund was received from centrally sponsored schemes, of which NREGS accounted for 84 per cent and IAY 6 per cent. (v) The rest was from PS, ZP, 12th Finance Commission, untied fund, etc. The above allocation patterns confirm an excessive fixation with the handed down schemes without which PRIs would have little to do and they may ultimately have to fold up.

A perusal of the records of the sample GPs disclosed that their activities mainly concerned community development and conferment of benefits to individuals. The community oriented activities—mostly under SGRY, NREGS and partly under finance commission and untied grants—included the following: construction, repair and renovation of kutcha and gravel road, rest shed, rooms for Anganwadi centres, SSK, excavation or repair of ponds and traditional water bodies, earth works of various types, plantation of trees, construction of crematorium, kitchen shed for primary school, repair of agricultural dam, provision for street light and piped water supply, promotion of SHG including help in asset creation, pound for stray animals, conduct of awareness camps as on agriculture, animal husbandry education, and engagement of doctors on contractual basis.

The community oriented activities strive for infrastructural development, livelihood security and civic facilities. While the infrastructural and asset creation efforts are going on for decades and some sort of tangible improvement has come by, the permissible works under the major development programmes are no less tied, as they have exclusive target group and specific purposes. Even NREGS is not open-ended, having a preordained list of allowable works. In the net, GPs can scarcely cater to what the villagers are now uniformly demanding, i.e., street light, piped drinking ware supply, pucca road, micro credit for self-employment ventures. Such hiatus and incapacity dampen the interest and desist the villagers from active participation in the village assembly meetings.[4]

The functional domain of GP evinces that decentralisation has taken the form of de-concentration and to an extent delegation but not devolution per se. Not surprisingly, the Report of the Third State Finance Commission (2008: 8) (of West Bengal) contends that the state government has not taken any formal step for devolution of functions to PRIs as required under the constitutional provisions as well as the panchayat act. Though PRIs are playing an increasing role in certain aspects of delivery, their ability to influence outcome has been limited, the reasons being the lack of clear allocation of responsibilities, inadequate access to discretionary funds, and lack of powers over state level functionaries and inadequate local capacity. Changing this scenario will involve systemic changes.

The villagers are not habitually apathetic to the community issues and stakes. The same villagers who remained indifferent to GS meetings had stood up and used GS and panchayat fora to force relocation of Thapar Dupont and Coca Cola Company so as to ensue safe environment and ground water level in the state of Goa and Tamil Nadu respectively. Villagers would take interest when GS can redress, at least partly, the collective problems or can attend to their major demands. For this to materialise, the functional domain of GP requires to be strengthened comprehensively. When GP does not have the capacity or wherewithal to consider or cater to the public demands, a bizarre situation envelops. Non-fulfilment of demands convinces villagers about non-responsiveness of GP members and they lose interest in GS meetings. At the same time, when GP members run the risk of being grilled for their perceived insensitivity, they try to avoid GS meetings. All lead to a predicament, typical to a political institution in the developing countries.

The public schemes offering benefits or addressing family contingencies include, IAY, Indira Gandhi National Old Age Pension (IGNOAP), Antyaodaya Anna Yojana (AAY), Annpurna Yojana, distribution of fertiliser, seed and pesticide to farmers and relief items to the distressed, provident fund for landless agricultural labourers as well as workers of unorganised sector and one-time grant to family under National Family Assistance Programme (NFAP).[5]

Selection of Beneficiary

GS is believed to be the most appropriate forum for selection of beneficiaries for the ongoing welfare schemes. This open and community platform is the best bet for need-based selection, for ensuring transparency and for setting right almost every wrong in beneficiary selection process. The public screening is expected to prevent personal or political favouritism, corruption and other types of misadventure or malfeasance. Many conceptual and structural vantage points notwithstanding, a positive role of GS in this regard is more easily said than done.

As the survey data have demonstrated (Chapter 3), the efficacy of Sansad in beneficiary selection is tenuous. Sansad did not, nor is likely to have great value and role in finally determining the recipients of scheme benefits. As most people attending the Sansad aspire for benefits and as there is galloping gaps between the public demands and availability of benefits, all aspirants cannot be saturated and this makes the final choice a tricky or abhorring one.

For years the common practice in West Bengal is that when a GP gets a specific number of quotas (for IAY, OAP, mini-kits) it distributes those among constituent wards (which ward gets what proportion depends on the bargaining power and political standing of the ward member). The selection of recipients for the available ward quotas is done almost uniformly at informal levels: for the CPM dominated ward/GP by the Booth (or *Sakha*) Committee members and for the Rightist party dominated ward/GP by few local level political leaders including the ward member. The list of candidatures compiled at informal level is usually presented to the Sansad and the list is ratified almost as the rule. The approval of Sansad may apparently authenticate the choice and voice of villagers but it is practically a mere endorsement without debate, acrimony or modification.

During and after the Sansad meeting one may come across two types of incidence. In odd occasions one or two members might assert in the meeting that really needy people have been excluded and comparatively affluent have got the benefits. The hidden story (strategy!) behind the championing of the deprivation of a few families may well be a political ploy where someone tries to build a rapport with the poor section or to vindicate that everything is not imposed from above or everything is not well and fine.

After meeting, few disgruntled persons might not be uncommon who murmur that they have not got the benefits as promised. Ironically though, they had been silent when the final list was approved without their names. One reason, as revealed, is that they cannot risk antagonising the political leadership by openly complaining their deprivation or breach of promise. They might have the opportunity but by daring to open complaining they would jeopardise the very prospect of securing whatever benefits that may come in future. By questioning the selection process, the villagers are more likely to invite displeasure or backlash of GP leadership.

The beneficiary selection process is not fair all the time. Many villagers at informal level pointed out (by mentioning name of recipients and the frequencies of benefit) how the 'comrades' (CPM panchayat leaders so regarded in North Bengal region) have usurped IAY benefits (construction and upgradation) and pump sets for minor irrigation. Regarding the quip why they did not protest or prevent such impropriety, villagers' logic veered around the common thread: "while in water, it is dangerous to attempt a fight with crocodile. We have to buy peace and live somewhat tranquilly, even if that is with hardship".

The party leadership is not always receptive to allegation or criticism. A pointed finger at the fault-lines evokes reaction and it is generally perceived as an attempt to affront or upstage the decision already made for the "poor" and all-round development. By raising question over ineligible intruders, thereby staking claim in those places, general people are more likely to be branded as those having been instigated by the opposition party or as those about to switch over political allegiance. Pressure to fall in line or face vengeance like denial of scheme benefit and social boycott are not uncommon. It is desirable that general villagers should be proactive in identifying and preventing anomalies in the selection of beneficiaries, but it is not easy for them. They can live without a tin shed, sanitary latrine or few hundred bucks a month but they can ill-afford the multiplying troubles consequent upon frowning on the preferences or decisions of the panchayat leadership.

Together with possible wrath or retribution, another noteworthy facet is that an individual initiative to ward off wrong selection of beneficiary or to expel the ineligible intruder is unlikely to succeed in a mass forum. Support of a sizeable section of the participants can help but the prospect of collectivity over individual-centric benefits is remotely realistic. The opposition political parties and community organisations have the wherewithal to take up the task more strongly and successfully. But the opposition party supporters hardly attend Sansad meetings. And the presence of community-based organisations is few and far between and they cannot also wish away the political pulls or consequences.

In the same vein, the political leadership plays an orchestrated role intending to sooth the public frustration and to drive home the lesson that scheme benefits will come only with its approval and sponsorship. It routinely informs the people that because of resource constraints and scheme-specific criteria, only very impoverished ones have been selected this time and many other excluded poor should not feel bereaved as they would certainly get benefits next time. By dangling the prospect of impending benefits and mouthing pro-poor posturing, public grievances are sought to be kept within a manageable limit.

The responses of respondents had indicted that whatever benefits they could gain was not the result of their initiative at Sansad forum and they did prefer to place their demands mainly to panchayat members and party leaders. Indeed, villagers favour parley with GP members, local party leaders at individual level and they find the informal channel more expedient and rewarding. They can meet, stake claim and pursue the case often repeatedly and together with fellow villagers or with recommendation of others. Alternatively, they can at best put forth their claim at Sansad but cannot explain their condition, convince others and impress the dispenser.

Nor GP members and party leaders prefer Sansad as the site for selecting beneficiaries. For the politicians the informal channel is more convenient to deal with the individual-centric demands. Allowing or facing those demands in open forum and at times rebutting or refusing such claims is not only embarrassing but also a politically dangerous proposition. At informal level they can maintain a patron-client relationship, tighten noose around the spate of demands or make a promise but in open forum everything can go overboard.

GS is seldom one suitable forum for finally choosing who among the participants would receive benefit and who would not. Any omission and commission on its part is likely to land GS into discountenance with the village folk. Knowledge and information about the economic conditions of the members is one thing but finally approving one at the expense of many others is no less onerous and perplexing task. When it is the question of individual benefit, a sense of sacrifice or fellow feeling on the part of a large section of participants is essential, but does it manifest or can it be expected in this 'self-aggrandising era'? Given the all-India trends, GS is finding itself trapped in indecision and is playing it safe by incorporating almost every eligible person in the approved list of beneficiaries and allowing the GP to take a final decision.

The one-line provision in most state panchayat acts—that GS will select beneficiaries—smacks of a casual treatment and rhetorical reference without grasping the practical underpinnings and impediments. Selection of beneficiaries is basically one embarrassing, thorny task and above all, it must precede a detailed and objective procedure. Kerala is perhaps the only state that has comprehended the issue and has provided for one logical modus operandi. GPs in Kerala first appraise the prescribed eligibility norms, priority and invite application from prospective beneficiaries which are then examined and short-listed by one smaller committee based on weightage given to specific criteria. GSs then prepare and forward to GP the priority list of individual/family for final distribution. This envisaged procedure is commendable and worth emulating as it retains the respective powers of GS and GP without dragging them into loggerhead, ensure relative transparency and need-based selection and keeps villagers and politicians contended.

No such specific procedure has been envisaged in West Bengal. Furthermore, the authority of Sansad over selection of deserving beneficiaries is getting constricted. The Rural Household Survey, 2005 has turned out to be an administrative attempt to chronicle objective and authentic socio-economic conditions of villagers and to direct development initiatives as per the categorisation of villagers drawing on the survey data. The survey collected data on 12 different indices, each with 5-point scale.[6] For instance, about the nature of the dwelling conditions indicator number two sought to document how many households are living (i) without having own homestead, (ii) with one kuchha room, (iii) with two or more kuchha rooms, (iv) with room partially pucca and (v) with rooms fully pucca. And based on the score of each household the Department of Panchayat has categorised households as belonging to, to use official code, P2=1, P2=2, P2=3, P2=4 and P2=5 disaggregated up to Sansad level. As per the instruction of the Department, those households befalling under P2=1 would first be considered for IAY. Permanent wait list for IAY (starting from the lowest and ending with highest scores of the eligible households like SC, ST, Minority and general category) will be prepared by the Block office. By now almost all P2=1 households have reportedly been offered house under IAY in most of the GPs and it is now the turn of P2=2 households.

What is noteworthy is that the survey data have been accepted as authentic and the basis on which almost everything will now revolve. In devising and compiling such an important index, the village assembly had not been informed or consulted and the administrative initiative undermined the voice of the people and discredited the otherwise vaunted eminence of the village assembly, which now has no option but to follow the listed positions of its members. Besides taking away the decision-making power of Sansad, the scores, ranks and categories have afforded yet another opportunity to GP members (and officials) to do all the preparatory work and at times to take final decision.

Assuming there is no sideway intervention or manipulation, the selection of beneficiaries now gets confined to the administratively graded households. As every villager may not have clear knowledge about the standing of others and as Sansad has no authority to select anyone who has been misplaced in the list, either inadvertently or otherwise, it effectively devolves on the GP members to shortlist eligible households and Sansad can only approve such listed candidatures in terms of available quota. It is ironical that in deciding such important issues like BPL or dwelling status Sansad has been bypassed and it can do nothing to correct wrong entries, if any. However, it is a different question that there are recurring complaints about the erroneous entries and rankings. Moreover, Sansad has now little role in selecting candidates for IGNOAP: its coverage has recently been extended as entitlement to all BPL people.

Party Control over Panchayat Process

When the structural ambiguities and fetters on functional domain of GP dampen the prospect of participation of people in the village assembly meetings, another weighty issue is the decision-making process of Gram Panchayat. A change from low intensity citizenship to substantial citizenship can be expected or impacted when the general people get a receptive ambience where their views are sought and valued. The quantitative aspect may create 'critical mass' in the long run, but the qualitative transformation can come by when people are encouraged in the deliberation and their viewpoints and demands are considered and incorporated in the decision-making.

It merits mention that the norms and culture of Indian politics are not very conducive to collective, transparent and responsive decision-making. The distance between the elected leaders and the led is widening sharply. The entrenching political and administrative culture treats people as seekers and receivers and the leaders as the givers in the form of 'pro-poor' policy and public dole. The elected representatives tend to regard themselves as special, powerful and masters. Particularly in rural India, the villagers-state relationship revolves more on the matrix of a gift economy rather than in the realm of rights and responsibilities (Rao and Sanyal, 2009: 16). Political parties engage themselves in the politics of patronage and maintenance of network to exchange public and private goods for electoral support. Manifested is the quid pro quo arrangement between vote maximising political parties and benefits maximising citizens (Majumdar, 2009: 93). In this overall context, does not the institution of GS seek to reverse the inverse relationship by subjecting and subordinating GP members to the general villagers and can GS easily be able to take the skewed process head on? Worth considering is the lessons gained from the working experience of Sansad and Sabha in West Bengal.

What makes PRIs in West Bengal exclusive is the political orientation and party control over the decision-making, petrified arguably to an unparalleled extent by the record rule of LFG and feeble presence and disorganised nature of the opposition parties. It should, however, be acquiesced that some sort of party control over PRIs is unmistakable throughout Indian states and it cannot be wished away. In fact, political calculations and exigencies are the decisive determinants that have promoted or prevented the evolution of panchayats.

Near unanimity is that LFG (read CPM) has promoted panchayats not for its ideological conviction to decentralisation or local democracy but specifically for political and electoral purposes: widening the support base among rural Bengal and as the countervailing institutional force against the resistance from the landed gentry and local bureaucracy to land reforms. CPM had been well aware of possible dangers coming out of panchayats. As Satyabrata Sen, one influential ideologue, perceived it: panchayat system is a sharp two-faced weapon. If you can use it properly it will turn into a sharp weapon for political mass movement. And if you cannot use it properly you yourself will bleed.[7]

While panchayats can play instrumental role in spreading and consolidating party organisation and support base among rural masses that hold the electoral key, it is possible that the emergence of the panchayat leadership may pose problem to the party leadership and policies—the usual apprehension in most states. It is equally probable that if rural people are allowed to assert themselves freely and squarely chances may be that the rationale for and conformity to the party policies may be challenged, the panchayat system may crumble because of overload of public demands and in that case the very system may be counterproductive. To minimise the "double jeopardy", two pronged strategy might have been devised. By withholding the autonomy, PRIs have been reduced to be mere agency of the state government and an extensive control mechanism has been woven so as to retain panchayats under the tight party strap.

The CPM party documents elaborate the party's conception and objectives of panchayats and these are certainly different from the liberal notion of democracy. Its attitude towards panchayats is instrumental and manipulative.[8] Panchayats are to be subservient to the authority of the party and be utilised for the party objectives. To the party, panchayats are to be used for the party purpose and not for any other *quo animo*.[9]

An extensive and powerful cobweb of party organisations has consequently been woven around each panchayat institution and important functionary. CPM's District Committee controls Zilla Parishad, Zonal Committee directs Panchayat Samity and Local Committee guides Gram Panchayat (Bhattacharyya, M., 2002: 168). Another structure evident in the North Bengal region is the *Pradhan Sahayak Committee* that, consisting of important party leaders of GP area, steers Pradhan and takes important GP level decisions like allocation of scheme quotas among GP wards, location of major schemes and fixing dates of Sansad and Sabha meetings. Though this committee is absolutely informal, its resolution books are openly available in GP office. In other words, those party organisations correspond to each tier command, control and supervise the panchayat decisions according to the directives of the party hierarchy and play crucial role in translating the perspective of the party.

Admittedly, such party commands prevent possible abuse of panchayat power, integrate as well as facilitate the realisation of the goals and policies of the state government and produce discipline and efficiency. They can also be advantageous for serving collective village interests, monitoring over programme implementation and for enforcing accountability. But these, at the same time, allow party functionaries to assume overriding role. Such centralisation of decision-making power in the hands of few party leaders not formally associated with PRIs tends to strike at the roots of democratic decentralisation in general and grassroots fora in particular. Panchayats then turn into a stooge of the ruling party leaders. The autonomy of action for GP (and other tier) members, who are to play the prime role in successful decentralisation, gets constricted and circumvented. When GP members themselves do not have control over panchayat decision-making, when villagers are well aware that the approval of the party leaders is the key to get anything done and when Sansad and Sabha meetings cannot take important decisions, some passivity to and futility of Sansad-like meetings is more likely. What then survives is the political value of participation. While the available evidences suggest little positive effects of decentralisation on popular participation and evolution of local democracy, institutionalisation of Sansad and

Sabha does not unequivocally promote participation of people in qualitative terms.

Party control over panchayats is a miniature of the larger design of 'political management'. CPM is said to have devised new rules of the game, has unleashed a new brand and axioms of politics in rural Bengal, substantially transforming the idioms of democracy.[10] In rural Bengal the political parties have emerged as the basic, elementary and all pervading institutions that have permeated and subsumed almost every socio-political organisation and even relations. The overarching parties subordinate, marginalise everything and inhibit free expression and persecute dissidents in Orwellian fashion. The parties, more so their local level leaders look after village governance, control socio-economic and cultural institutions, assist villagers in overcoming contingencies, they arbitrate social, familial and personal disputes at inter-personal levels—often touted as the glorious functions of Bengal's panchayats.

What has eventually come about is regarded as the 'party society', one special form of political society where political parties have assumed guardianship of villagers' public and even private lives and where the conventional channels of public transaction have been usurped by the parties (Bhattacharyaa, 2009: 60).[11] In this new form of transaction, the organisational grid of party has become the main mediator, the central conduit for deciding and settling village level issues (Chatterjee, 2009: 43). If this framework and precepts have been precipitated by CPM, other parties are following suit, to the extent possible for them.[12]

PRIs have played strategic role in solidifying the ethos of the party society. Because of the very nature of panchayat activities, parties have found it easy to extend hold and entangle poor villagers in particular. Panchayats all along have pronounced welfare bias where most schemes are beneficiary oriented. Emphasis on consumption instead of asset creation or investment affords the allocation pattern of expenditure where individual or family happens to be the unit. This frame offers considerable scope to parties for patronage or clientelism and thereby binds the benefit seekers to the tethers of the party.

Panchayats have reinforced the dominant role of the parties in guiding development and distribution of public benefits. Such party ascendancy diminishes the prospect of unmediated popular initiative and spontaneous participation of people insulated from the endorsement or approval of the party leaders. Thus some sort of 'paradox' unfurls. Decentralisation may have offered the opportunity, yet the rural people do not get easy and unencumbered access to panchayat decision-making or to direct the course of local development because the organised electoral (and vested) interests of the ruling party arbitrate everything.[13] Earlier villagers had to depend on the *jotedar*, moneylenders and now they come under the clutches of the party leaders.

Surely, the involvement and intermediary role of the party leaders and activists has some positive impacts on the targeting and distribution of public schemes to the deserving sections. But the better records regarding disbursement of welfare fund is least related to the participation of and direction from the village people. When panchayats are mere delivery mechanism and they implement public schemes relatively efficiently and without considerable corruption, leakage or target failure, some sort of managerial efficiency may be undeniable, but this is at the expense of capacity building of the stakeholders and fulfilment of the ideals of participatory democracy.

Intrinsic to and as a corollary of the 'party society', the ruling party supporters are mobilised for Sansad and Sabha meetings and, not surprisingly, the participants attend somewhere with party flags. Such partisan orientation has two offshoots. *Firstly*, when the non-ruling party supporters stay away (their presence in a single party dominated GP is looked down upon suspiciously), Sansad and Sabha meetings fail to register the community representation. When the societal character is gobbled up by the party leviathan, Sansad and Sabha turn into party Sansad and party Sabha. *Secondly*, the almost exclusive congregation of the ruling party supporters is expected to act as Milton's angels and to appreciate and approve whatever the leadership says or places before them. This phenomenon staves off the possibility of adverse or uncomfortable questions. The ostensible objective of the meeting is then to appraise and convince the participants about the commitment of the leadership to the common weal and emphatic development initiatives being hastened within the squeezed functional and financial periphery.

Surely, some participants speak out in village assembly meetings but their contents are controlled, if not manipulated—quiet easily when the participants belong to the same party orbit. The Pradhan, in particular, tries to hijack the major demands of the villagers and attempts to act on behalf of the villagers. He routinely furnishes details of the ongoing development activities, schemes already submitted to the higher levels and demands immediate sanctions and speedy commencement of those proposed scheme works. This strategy pre-empts the possible demands coming from the villagers. Emphasis is on those issues and problems which concern the majority of the community people. Individual level deprivations or inconveniencies are allowed to be vented to an extent and the opportunity is skilfully used to promise redress, to inform the incapacity arising out of constraints beyond control or non-cooperation of the villagers (tax arrears, land for NREGS), thus publicly proving the 'pro-people' leaning and sustaining the importance and legitimacy of the elected representatives of GP.

Whatever the participants express or seek has only ceremonial value; it does not have much insinuation into the decision and activities of GP. The public views and demands are not officially incorporated in the final resolution of the meeting. Whoever takes the final decision, it is far away from the public glare. Sansad plays no significant role in selecting beneficiary, picking or choosing development schemes, monitoring or evaluating programme implementation or in formulating much hyped village development plan. Sansad is yet to evolve as the collective decision-making platform or exercising approval or recommending functions.

When the powerful groups like large landowners exert an unduly large influence on the deliberative and decision-making process of GS meetings (Ban and Rao, 2009: 20), when GS is hardly a place of deliberative democracy where the participants, whatever is the quantity, get engaged in rational negotiation to reach consensus with single peaked preferences (Rao and Sanyal, 2009: 36), when GS is more a forum where discursive competition for garnering a piece of the public pie or for staking claim to the gift of the state is evident, when GS evolves, as in Kerala, as one mechanism for legitimising the 'authoritarian consensus formed by the party leaders',[14] the overall situation in West Bengal is not fundamentally contrasting. Sansad and Sabha meetings are more like party meetings without the involvement of non-ruling party supporters, a talking and reporting forum without having substantial sequel except maintaining or forming legitimacy for panchayat institution and representatives. When political motives determine people's participation the community credibility collapses, when development decisions are not taken through open deliberation and dithering the efficacy suffers. Democratic deficits distend when without express approval of the participants and without the consent of the cross-sections, the preferences and priorities of a few are extended to be of the entire village community.

Seen in overall perspective and to put it tersely, GS, in generic sense, is akin to one colourful balloon that has been designed somewhat casually, infused with air composed of high expectations, allowed to float in the wilderness and hard hit, if not punctured, by the missiles of party politics. If such an impression provokes panchayat-*wallas*, the fact remains that the first incarnation of the statutory GS had failed miserably and its second innings since 1993 seems equally disquieting. Yet, this village assembly should not be regarded as the villain or one fallen angel. The onus should be apportioned more by the deficient design, inordinate hype and insurmountable dynamics of panchayat politics. More perspicuity rather than objectivity tends to be the order of the day. GS could have been spared from the ignominies if its powers were consistent with the capacity and the euphoria surrounding it was pragmatic. GS cannot but traverse its course within the norms and bounds of panchayat as well as party politics. And there is little justifiable reason to believe that the faux pas would evaporate with the growing maturity of the villagers and endowment of authoritative powers. The expectation that GS would be one unique institution free from the general malaises and it would rectify the deficits of Indian democracy seems presumptuous.

Notes and References

1. Letter of Ministry of Panchayati Raj, Government of India, dated 2 October, 2009, requesting the states to observe 2009–10 as the Year of Gram Sabha.
2. Only about 6 per cent of total revenues of GPs is derived from own source of revenue and 94 per cent comes from grants and transfers, of which 70 per cent is from Central Government and 24 per cent from State Government [*Report of the Third State Finance Commission*, (2008: 27), submitted to government of West Bengal].

   Raising own source of revenue has been one detesting proposition mainly for the political risks involved and administrative incapacity. How far the situation can improve if GS is given the power to levy taxes and enhance the rates is doubtful. Under *Gram Swaraj* in Madhya Pradesh, where Manor (2001) foresaw a breakthrough, the scenario did not improve much: as per the Second State Finance Commission Report, 2003, 55 per cent of the sample GPs raised no tax revenue, 70 per cent raised no non-tax revenue and 46 per cent GPs did not raise any revenue whatsoever.
3. To one account, out of total 666 major village development schemes, 477 are handled exclusively by the line agencies of the state government and 58 (mostly centrally sponsored) by GP. Over 59 schemes the line departments share some powers with GP (Khasnabis Ratan, 2008. *Disquieting Record of Devolution to Panchayats*. Paper presented in the International Conference on 'Three Decades of Rural Decentralisation in West Bengal: Lessons and Future Options', organised by Institute of Social Sciences and held in Kolkata on 12–13 December.)

4. If the present functional domain is not buoyant, its restructuring is not in the offing. In order to provide due authority to GPs, of course by not reducing the responsibilities of the state, one recent document (GoWB, 2009, *Roadmap for the Panchayats*) has proposed that GPs will have *regulatory* function over, inter alia, giving permission to construction of structure, building, assessment and collection of taxes, rates and fees, registration of vehicles, trucks, shallow, maintenance of street light and *complementary* function (as an agency) over generation of awareness among people on their role in preparation of plan, livelihood opportunity, campaign against social evil.
5. There are other welfare schemes like pension for widow, old age pension to fishermen, artisans, tribal and disability pension schemes being implemented by line Department or Ministry.
6. Household having scores below 33 (earlier <28), out of maximum 60, are listed as living Below Poverty Line.
7. Quoted by Budhadeb Bhattacharya in his interview to *People's Democracy*, July 4, 2004.
8. Bhattacharyya, Harihar (1998: 104). *Micro-Foundation of Bengal Communism*, New Delhi: Ajanta.
9. As one party document spelt it out unequivocally: "democratic participation does not mean acting at will. It means that the activation of panchayats in accordance with the principles of and ideals of the party. The basic issue involved here is giving party leadership to panchayats. ... The political leadership of the party is established only when people in their own experience accept the political perspective of the party as their own. The party has a definite aim. Panchayats activities should be conducted in such a way that conforms to the basic goals of the party" (Quoted in Chakraborty, Bidyut (2006: 3623). 'Left Front's 2006 Victory in West Bengal', *Economic & Political Weekly*, August 12, 2006.)
10. CPM's engagement with democracy in West Bengal is alleged to be quite contrasting. It champions democracy when not in power but when in the saddle it follows moderate fascism whose ingredients are 'Marxist ideology, Leninist party and Stalinist state'. Criticism or opposition to left ideology and programmes is seen as an attempt to refute the 'historical truth'.

Independent view is strangulated, autonomy for social groups is untenable and this paves way for general inertia, conformity and a sense of resignation among masses (Mukherjee, Sanjeeb, 2007. 'The Use and Abuse of Democracy in West Bengal', *Economic & Political Weekly*, November 3, 101–108.)

11. Or to use the metaphor of Lieten (1996: 183), the party leadership is the stem while the villagers are the frittering leaves depending on the stem for sustenance.
12. For successful role performance of GS the suggestions that GP members should show patience, tolerance, accommodative spirit and they should allow popular voice and concede decision-making power to villagers have to be posited on this broader frame.
13. Gent, John Echeverri, 1992. 'Politics of Development and the Development of Politics: An Inquiry into the Political Means of Equitable Development,' *Contemporary South Asia*, 1 (3), 325–349.
14. Moolakkattu, Stephen, John, and Kunhambu, V.V, 2005. 'People's Participation in Gram Sabha: Evidence from Three Village Panchayats in Malabar (Kerala)', *Man & Development*, 27 (2), June.

Appendices

Appendix 1

Seat share of Major Political Parties in West Bengal Panchayat Institutions (Figures in rounded of percentage)

	Gram Panchayat				*Panchayat Samity*				*Zilla Parishad*			
Year	*Total Seats*	*LF*	*CPM*	*Oppo-sition*	*Total Seats*	*LF*	*CPM*	*Oppo-sition*	*Total Seats*	*LF*	*CPM*	*Oppo-sition*
1978	46845	70	61	30	8467	77	67	23	648	90	77	10
1983	46153	61	54	39	8684	66	60	34	678	75	69	25
1988	52520	72	65	28	9128	79	72	21	658	90	81	10
1993	61010	64	58	36	9453	73	67	27	656	87	81	13
1998	49199	56	50	44	8515	67	61	33	716	88	78	12
2003	49140	66	58	34	8500	74	67	26	713	87	77	13
2008	41504	52	46	48	8800	56	49	44	748	69	61	31

LF: All Constituents of Left Front, CPM: Communist Party of India (Marxist), Opposition: All non-Left Parties.

Appendix 2

People's Attendance in Gram Sansad Meetings (District-wise)

District	Total Sansad	Total members	May, 2002			November, 2002		
			Meeting held (%)	Total attendance (%)	Women's attendance (%)	Meeting held (%)	Total attendance (%)	Women's attendance (%)
Cooch Behar	1701	749	82	17	3	58	19	2
Jaipaiguri	2095	744	98	18	2	87	19	2
Uttar Dinajpur	1470	740	100	9	1	99	10	2
Dakshin Dinajpur	925	744	100	7	1	100	9	2
Malda	2021	738	86	9	1	75	9	1
Murshidabad	3614	784	97	18	NA	87	6	NA
Nadia	2639	798	97	10	2	98	10	2
Uttar 24 pargana	2923	761	97	10	2	87	7	2
Dakshin 24 pargana	4324	769	99	8	2	54	12	2
Howrah	2218	803	99	6	1	45	6	1
Hoogly	3001	801	100	11	2	82	11	2
Purba Midnapur	2970	804	99	12	3	94	12	4
Paschim Midnapur	3449	787	99	11	2	80	18	3
Bankura	2488	750	97	9	1	72	4	1
Purulia	1925	711	97	11	1	68	11	1
Bardhaman	3833	817	99	12	3	48	11	2
Bibhum	2108	764	94	8	1	NA	NA	NA

Source: Panchayati Raj Samachar, November, 2002 and January–February, 2003.

Appendix 2, continued

Meeting of Gram Sabha in West Bengal

Year	No. of Gram Sabha	Average elector per Gram Sabha	Gram Sabha Meeting Held with Quorum (%)	People's Attendance in Gram Sabha Meeting (%)
1999	3330	9985	89	5.5
2000	3360	10015	92	5
2001	3360	10093	75	NA
2002	3358	8370	58	5
2003	3354	9664	90	7
2007	3242	NA	72	NA

Source: Annual Administrative Report, 2003–04—2008–09, Department of Panchayat and Rural Development, Government of West Bengal.

Appendix 3

People's Attendance in Special Gram Sansad Meetings (for formation of GUS)

Booth No.	*Date of Meeting*	*Total Voter*	*Member Present*	*% to Total Voter*	*Members Elected*
		Andaran Fulbari Gram Panchayat I			
24	6–3–2005	914	210	23	20
25	13–3–2005	1435	198	14	17
27	12–3–2005	1393	254	18	23
28	8–3–2005	857	169	20	17
29	11–3–2005	913	213	23	20
30	9–3–2005	1427	248	17	22
		Andaran Fulbari Gram Panchayat II			
21	27–4–2005	867	124	14	19
22	29–4–2005	774	207	27	18
23	24–3–2005	696	176	25	20
24	27–3–2005	864	184	21	19
25	5–4–2005	615	437	71	22
26	31–3–2005	873	203	23	16
27	24–3–2005	891	203	23	19
30	20–3–2005	723	140	19	16

Source: Official records of the Gram Panchayats.

Appendix 4

Sansad Meeting: a Live Account

We had personally attended three Sansad meetings of different GPs of Cooch Behar (Koch Bihar) and Murshidabad district and recorded the proceedings in order to get first-hand information or to feel the pulse, literally. In those meetings we have found basic similarities pertaining to the extent of participation of villagers, GP members and officials, the points of speaking by dignitaries and villagers. The attendance of people was thin, the topic of discussion revolved around revised BPL list and NREGS works and villagers, broadly, clamoured over inclusion of their names in BPL list. The discussion on development schemes was either casual or put to a back-bench. No resolution of meeting was formally adopted or approved. We reproduce below the proceeding of Sansad meeting of Booth (ward) No. 24 of Andaran Fulbari II GP of Cooch Behar (Koch Bihar) as one typical instance of what transpires in a Sansad meeting. The description is slightly abridged and edited for the sake of sequence and relevancy but it is verbatim for the GP members (with free translation).

Sansad meeting was first slated on 12 December, 2008 but it had to be adjourned due to lack of quorum. The reconvened meeting was held on 18 December. The Pradhan, two GP staff and the elected ward member arrived together around 4.50 PM. The venue was the open ground in front of one ICDS centre. A long plastic sheet was laid on the ground for sitting purpose and one plastic type tarpaulin was erected with bamboo structure over the ground to prevent winter fogging. One temporary dais was arranged with two tables, six plastic chairs. Two bulbs were lit with one battery: one in front of dais and other for the podium. Villagers began to pour in one by one from around 5 PM and the meeting started at 5.35, 65 minutes behind schedule, and it continued for about two hours. Only about 46 members (21 women) were present during the start of the meeting and some others joined later on. Just before dispersal we head-counted total 47 male and 34 female participants, though the attendance register filled up by one local youth (not attached to GP but close to ward member) showed total 106 members (out of total 900). Interestingly, the elected ward member happened to be the Pradhan of the GP for three consecutive terms and when after 2008 elections the

CPM lost control of GP power (to TMC) for the first time ever, this ward returned the lone CPM member in the GP. Because of the long association of the elected ward member, his unaltered political support and his present minority position in the GP board, this Sansad meeting was expected to demonstrate a high degree of people's attendance, protracted struggle over political support-base and the observation of the ward member was to unfold the nuances that Sansad is likely to entail.

The Pradhan, after consulting elected ward member and GP staff rose from the chair and started the meeting with the following words: "in this meeting ... persons (name and designation) are present. I welcome all the participants. This is one adjourned meeting. As you know, the earlier meeting was to be adjourned because sufficient number of people did not turn up that time. This is one unfortunate event. You should not be apathetic to but be interested in Sansad meeting. Sansad is yours, the entire villagers. This is one important forum for you, where you should come and know the developmental activities being undertaken by the Gram Panchayat, about the future programmes to be taken up for your booth and other areas. In this forum you would be able to voice your concerns, demands and we would try to take care and fulfil those to the best of our capacity and fund availability. In this forum you would guide us, indicate the lapse in our initiatives and inform us what is essential for you. Also, we are legally bound to hold two Sansad meetings every year. If we do not follow this legal prescription, the government will sanction no development fund. In that case you will be deprived of basic services and facilities. Now the budget and audit reports will be presented and you are requested to place your views and demands after the presentation".

Then the GP *Karmee* began to read out from a two-page typed paper for about 17 minutes. He first spelt out the estimated income of GP from several heads and then the possible expenditure under the similar heads. The subject matters of the Report were technical, the reading style was tedious and the villagers did not make any comment whatsoever during and after the presentation.

Thereafter, the Job Assistant of GP presented the audit report for the year 2007–08. He first spoke about the importance of and the procedure for audit: particularly the significant shift in auditing first by Panchayat Accounts Officer and now by the chartered accountant firm short-listed by the Department of Panchayat. He specifically took up few points over which the auditor commented adversely and explained in details the reasons for and the position of GP thereon. He first picked up the comment of auditor regarding the negligible own tax revenue collection, huge tax arrears, unaltered assessment rates for land and buildings and the recommendation for the concerted and immediate effort to inflate the coffer of GP so as to undertake development works as per the priorities of the people. He elucidated that the tax arrears are due to the evasion and insensitivity of the tax payers themselves. Moreover, GP could not increase the assessment rates all of a sudden and abnormally without the consent and cooperation of the villagers. In essence, he sought to clarify that without the active gesture and collaboration of villagers, GP cannot realise tax arrears, increase tax base and in that case GP will continue to draw flak from auditors in future as well.

The Job Assistant further dwelt on the comment of the auditor regarding few idle bank accounts. He informed that those accounts were for specific scheme works and as those schemes are not presently in operation no transaction could be made thereon. GP would in its next meeting adopt resolution for closing those inoperative accounts, he informed.

Next he singled out the comment that development programmes like installation of electric connection and street light were not implemented even though GP had adopted resolution accordingly. The Job Assistant reported that the delay was due to wrangling between government Departments and on this front GP cannot do much in hastening the project works.

The Job Assistant delved long into the comment of the auditor on NREGS. The auditor reportedly indicated that GP took up only few schemes and the man-days so created were scanty and much could have been done. The Job Assistant informed that though the criticism is valid the deficiency is not squarely due to the negligence on the part of GP but to the typical geographical nature of the areas and scheme guidelines. He elaborated on the point that as this GP is adjacent to a sub-divisional town the dwellings are dense, price of land is high and there is hardly any free or vested land. As per NREGS guidelines, every proposed scheme ought to entail the plot (*dag*) number of the land on which the works are to be carried on. Thus, without the willing consent of the owners of the land it was not possible to frame or furnish any scheme such as road building, social forestry, pond digging or minor irrigation. "Do you provide land, are you willing to offer land for public purpose? If you do not give us land, how we can propose, execute scheme works and give you works", he quipped. Another dimension was that there is virtually no wet land or vested land in the areas, whatever was available had already been used for social forestry. For pond digging or minor irrigation scheme, one bottleneck was that no such work can be proposed on agricultural land. One way out could be to convert agricultural land into wet land. But "such conversion is time consuming, if not impossible, as many procedural hurdles are to be overcome and formal certificate from DL&LRO is to be obtained. He almost explicitly hinted that villagers should not expect more NREGS works in coming months.

Thereafter, the elected ward member delivered a long lecture where he narrated the status of few programmes, the reasons for their fumbling and his incapacity to accommodate new families in the BPL list. Indeed he started with a lamentation and concluded with an urge to make Sansad a success.

In his own word: (after introduction of the persons at the dais by names) This is one adjourned meeting. Earlier meeting was postponed as required number of members did not turn up. The number of members is not encouraging this time also. This morning I toured the booth area and requested almost all families to come to Sansad. Yet your presence is not heartening. You should come forward and make Sansad a success for your own sake.

I know the reason of your lukewarm response, the frustration of the villagers of this booth. You feel deprived and disgruntled as scores of genuinely deserving families do not find their names in the revised BPL list. It is unbelievable that only 23 families (out of total 400) have been enlisted while the number should have been not less than 150. I can feel your agony and anger. I have taken up your concerns with block officials and even with District Magistrate. Not only in this and other booths of this GP but also in other GPs, similar anomalies are piling up. We, the panchayat members are consistently conveying your indignation to the higher officials who are also pleading their helplessness without government instruction for revision of the list. As you know, the BPL list is based on the data compiled from the Rural Household Survey, 2005. The Block office did the survey, engaging primary school teachers. During the survey we repeatedly inquired from officials about the intent of the survey and they told us that this is yet another survey and nothing else. As such, you and I did not have any inkling about the motive of the survey. For this reason you might have answered questions casually, somewhere exceedingly. Also the surveyors might not have visited every hearth or collected authentic information from every household. Somewhere, they might have collected information about the entire *para* from a few villagers and treated those inputs genuine. This may be one reason why even the destitutes are excluded from the list.

... Recently BDO has informed me that in view of repetition of many family names, minor modification in the BPL list may be possible and he has given me few forms for filling up. But I am in a fix. As the number of deserving families is enormous and forms are few, to which families I should give forms is one difficult choice for me.

Inadequate work opportunity under NREGS, lack of street light and scanty irrigation facilities are few problems of this booth. The Electricity Department has recently made survey works and some work is expected soon. The pump house is in a dilapidated condition and electric connection is not presently available there. The engineer of Zilla Parishad has approved its renovation and reinstallation of electric connection. The designated contractor has already visited the spot and he is about to start the work.

Yes, the work opportunities under NREGS are insufficient, compared to the demands of the villagers. But it would be difficult for this GP to open up avenues for substantial works. As the Job Assistant (by name) already informed you, the scheme guidelines are constricting in nature. Most of the permissible schemes are land related. But available or free land is the problem that is halting the initiative of this GP. Neither land is freely available nor are you voluntarily willing to provide land for public purpose. The scarcity of land is the problem not only for this and other booths but also for nearby GPs and for this reason you cannot easily be accommodated in works in other places. Some of you might have got works for few days in the construction of market complex (in separate booth, expending ₹ 8 lakh). We, in the GP, decided to engage workers for this market complex work proportionately from each GP booth. One result of this decision was that only a few of you could actually get work. Another difficulty you faced was the late payment of wage bill. Those of you who have account in bank might have received payment within a month but those having accounts in post office could not get it for about two months. For this delay and inconvenience we are helpless. We forwarded the invoice but the post office took time to cash it ....

Panchayat is the executive agency of the government. The state government delegates (*nastya*) funds for development works. And we have to implement programmes according to the prescribed rules and procedures. We cannot flout such rules. You have variegated demands and problems and you are expected to put those in Sansad meetings. We would certainly try to satisfy your demands. But you should also remember that your every demand cannot be met or GP cannot saturate your claims instantly. The programmes have to be available, criteria to be followed, discussion with and concurrence of government Departments are to be obtained and only thereafter the work can commence. We do not undertake development works based on "political consideration" only. Neither can GP do it. This GP is constrained by norms and procedures (as in BPL list). You may sometimes feel aggrieved and put blame on us but we do convey your pent up feelings and concerns to the government officials.

Please come to Sansad meetings regularly and en masse. It is your forum. You can give us advice, submit your problems and indicate our fault-lines. Your participation is not only desirable but also imperative because without you GP is nothing. Remember, without resolution being adopted at Sansad no development programme or scheme work can legally be proposed, forwarded or executed. We may not always be able to redress or solve all you problems and demands but the occasional interaction with you would keep the GP activities people-centric. Now you submit your points of view, problems of this booth. And we will note those in the resolution of this Sansad.

After the speech of the ward member, many people, including women, pointed out their exclusion from the BPL list. Especially one older widow narrated her plight in a sharp tone, to which the ward member replied that he is well aware of her conditions and would try to see what he can do (*dakhee ke karte paree*). Then the ward member requested participants to come forward one by one and asked the GP *Karmee* to note down their names. Not in an orderly but in a scrambled fashion, participants gathered near the podium and GP *Karmee* included their names on a piece of paper. In the meantime two middle aged males came near to the dais and began venting their frustration. At that the ward member requested them to say their points facing the audience. Complying, they, one by one, recounted their predicament and urged inclusion of their names in the BPL list.

It took about 30 minutes to note down all the names of people. After that, the youth who earlier took attendance of people began to read out from a prepared list the names of the family head (altogether 131) that deserve to be included in BPL list. During the reading, villagers did not make any comment nor was there any clamouring. It was unclear whether the newly added names were already in the prepared list. However, it was gathered from the Job Assistant that the same family names were read out in the earlier meeting. Thereafter, the Pradhan thanked all the participants and others and concluded the meeting (of course, without mentioning or approving the resolution of this meting).

Bibliography

Administrative Reforms Commission, the Second, 2007. *Local Governance: an Inspiring Journey into the Future*. Department of Administrative Reforms and Public Grievances, New Delhi: Government of India.

Alsop, Ruth, Krishna and Sjoblom, 2000. 'Are Gram Panchayat Inclusive? Report of a Study Conducted in Rajasthan and Madhya Pradesh'. Background Paper No 3, in *Overview of Rural Decentralisation in India*. Vol. III. Washington: The World Bank.

Aziz, Abdul and Arnold, David, 1996. *Decentralised Governance in Asian Countries*. New Delhi: Sage.

Ban, Radu and Rao Vijayendra, 2009. *Is Deliberation Equitable? Evidence from Transcripts of Village Meetings in South India.* Washington: The World Bank, Development Research Group, Policy Research Working Paper No. 4928.

Banerjee, Chakravarty Sonali, 2002. *Social Background of Panchayat Leaders in West Bengal.* Kolkata: Dasgupta & Co.

Banerjee, Parthasarathi and Roy, Deyabati, 2005. *Gram Banglar Rajniti* (in Bengali). Kolkata: People's Book Society.

Bardhan, Pranab, 2002. 'Decentralisation of Governance and Development.' *Journal of Economic Perspective*, 16 (4), 185–205.

Bardhan, Pranab, Mitra, Mookherjee and Sarkar, 2009. 'Local Democracy and Clientelism: Implications for Political Stability in Rural West Bengal. *Economic & Political Weekly*, 28 February, 46–58.

Behar, Amitava, 2003. 'Experiment with Direct Democracy: Time for Reappraisal'. *Economic & Political Weekly*, May 17, 1925–1927.

Bhargava and Raphael, 1994. 'Working of Gram Sabha in Karnataka. A Study at Micro Level'. *Journal of Rural Development*, 13 (2), 145–157.

Bhattacharya, Moitree, 2002. *Panchayati Raj in West Bengal: Democratic Decentralisation or Democratic Centralisation*. New Delhi: Manak.

Bhattacharyya, Dwaipayan, 2009. 'Of Control and Factions: The Changing 'Party Society' in Rural West Bengal'. *Economic & Political Weekly*, February 28, 59–69.

——, 2006. 'Writers' Buildings and the Reality of Decentralised Rural Power', *in* Joyal, Prakash and Sharma, eds.

Bhattacharyya, Harihar, 2002. *Making Local Democracy Work in India*. New Delhi: Vedams Book.

Blair, H., 2000, 'Participation and Accountability at the Periphery: Democratic Local Governance in Six Countries'. *World Development*, 28(1), 21–39.

Chakraborthy, K. and Bhattacharyya, S., 1993. *Leadership, Factions and Panchayati Raj*, Jaipur: Rawat.

Chatterjee, Partha, 2009. 'The Coming Crisis in West Bengal'. *Economic & Political Weekly*, February 28, 42–45.

——, 2004. *The Politics of Governed; Reflection on Popular Politics in Most of the World*. New Delhi: Permanent Black.

Chatterjee, Rakhahari, ed., *Politics in West Bengal: Institution, Process and Problems*, Calcutta: World Press.

Chathukulam and John, 2002. 'Five Year of Participatory Planning in Kerala: Rhetoric and Reality'. *Economic & Political Weekly*, December 7.

Choudhury, R.C. and Jain, eds, 1999. *Strengthening Village Democracy*. Hyderabad: National Institute of Rural Development.

Conyers, Diana, 2008. *Deepening Democracy in the UK: Rhetoric and Reality*, Working Paper No 314. Brighton: Overseas Development Institute.

Corbridge, S. and Harriss, J., 2001. *Reinventing India: Liberalization, Hindu Nationalism and Popular Democracy*. New Delhi: Oxford University Press.

Corbridge, Stuard, Williams, Venor and Srivastava, 2003. 'Making Social Science Matter. How the Rural Poor See the State in Bihar, Jharkhand and West Bengal'. *Economic & Political Weekly*, 14 and 21 June, 2377–2389 and 2561–2569.

Costa, Dia Da, 2007. 'Tensions of Neo-Liberal Development: State Discourse and Dramatic Opposition in West Bengal'. *Contribution to Indian Sociology*, 41 (3), 287–320.

Crook, R.C. and Manor, J., 1998. *Democracy and Decentralisation in South Asia and West Africa*. Cambridge: Cambridge University Press.

Crook, R.C. and Sverrisson, A. Sturla, 2001. *Decentralisation and Poverty Alleviation in Developing Countries: a Comparative Analysis or, is West Bengal Unique?* IDS Working Paper No. 130. Brighton: Institute of Development Studies (IDS).

Dasgupta, Rajarshi, 2009. 'The CPI(M) 'Machinery' in West Bengal: Two Village Narratives from Kochbihar and Malda'. *Economic & Political Weekly*, February 28, 70–81.

Datta and Sen, Bhattacharyya, 2000. 'Participatory Rural Governance in India'. *Indian Journal of Public Administration*, 48(1), 38–49.

Debroy, Bibek and Kaushik, P.D., eds, 2004. *Emerging Rural Development Through Panchayat*. New Delhi: Academic Foundation.

Deshpande, S.V. and Murthy, Venkatesha G.B., 2002. 'Pressures from Below: Decentralised Governance in Karnataka'. *Economic & Political Weekly*, May 4, 1766–67.

Fernandes, Aurelliano, 2003. 'Aggrandiser Government Versus Local Governance'. *Economic & Political Weekly*, July 5.

——, 1999. 'Reconnecting Sabha to Gram', in Choudhury and Jain eds.

Franda, Marcus, 1971. *Political Development and Political Decay in Bengal*. Calcutta; Firma KLM.

Fung, Archon and Wright, Eric Olin, 2003. *Deepening Democracy: Institutional Innovations in Empowered Participatory Governance*. London: Verso.

——, 2001. 'Deepening Democracy: Innovations in Empowered Participatory Governance'. *Politics and Society*, 29(1), 5–41

Gaiha, Raghav and Kulkarni, Vani, 2002. 'Panchayats, Communities, and the Rural Poor in India'. *Journal of Asian and African Studies*, 37 (2), 38–82.

Ganguly, Sumit, Diamond, Larry and Plattner, Marc, eds, 2007. *The State of India's Democracy*. Baltimore: Johns Hopkins University Press (also Oxford University Press).

Gaventa, John, 2006. *Triumph, Deficit or Contestation? Deepening the 'Deepening Democracy' Debate*. Working Paper No 264, Brighton: Overseas Development Institute.

Ghatak M. and Ghatak. M, 2002. 'Recent Reforms in the Panchayat System in West Bengal.' *Economic & Political Weekly*, January 5, 45–58

Ghosh, Budhadeb and Kumar, Girish, 2003. *State Politics and Panchayats in India*. New Delhi: Manohar.

Goel, S.L. and Rajneesh, 2002. *Panchayat Raj in India: Theory and Practice*. New Delhi: Deep & Deep.

Government of India (GoI), 1963. *Report of the Study Team on the Position of Gram Sabha in Panchayati Raj Movement*. New Delhi: Ministry of Community Development and Cooperation (popularly known as Diwankar Committee report).

——, 1978. *Report of the Committee on Panchayati Raj Institutions*. New Delhi: Ministry of Agriculture and Irrigation (popularly known as Ashok Mehta Committee report).

——, 1999. *Report of the Sub Group of the Task Force on Panchayati Raj-Empowerment of Gram Sabha*. New Delhi: Ministry of Rural Development.

——, 2011. *Roadmap for the Panchayati Raj (2011–16); An All India Perspective*. New Delhi: Ministry of Rural Development.

Government of Rajasthan, 2001. *Report of the Administrative Reforms Commission on Panchayati Raj in Rajasthan*. Jaipur.

Government of West Bengal (GoWB), 2009. *Roadmap for the Panchayats in West Bengal: A Vision Document*. Kolkata: Panchayat and Rural Development Department.

——, 2001 to 2009, Panchayat and Rural Development Department, *Annual Administrative Report*, Kolkata.

Gupta, Monobina, 2010. *Left Politics in Bengal*, Hyderabad: Orient Black Swan.

Hadiz, Vedi, R., 2007. 'The Localization of Power in Southeast Asia.' *Democratization*, 14 (5), 873–892.

Harriss, John, Stokke, Kristian and Tornquist Olle, eds, 2004. *Politicising Democracy: The New Local Politics of Democratisation*. Palgrave: Macmillan.

Heller, P., 2001. 'Moving the State. The Politics of Democratic Decentralization in Kerala, South Africa, and Porto Alegre'. *Politics and Society*, 29 (1), 131–63.

Houtzager, Peter P., Lavalle, Adrián Gurza and Acharya, Arnab, 2003. *Who Participates? Civil Society and the new Democratic Politics in São Paulo, Brazil*, Working Paper 210. Brighton: Overseas Development Institute.

Human Development Report (HDR), *West Bengal*, 2004. Kolkata: Development and Planning Department, Government of West Bengal.

Issac, Thomas and Franke, Richard, 2000. *Local Democracy and Development*. New Delhi: Leftword.

Jain, L.C., ed., 2005. *Decentralisation and Local Governance*. New Delhi: Orient Longman.

Jain, S.P., 2002. *Gram Sabha: A Study of Two States*. Research Report Series no. 44. Hyderabad: National Institute of Rural Development.

——, ed., 2001. *Emerging Institutions for Decentralised Rural Development*. Hyderabad: National Institute of Rural Development.

——, 1997. 'Gram Sabha: Gateway to Grassroots Democracy', *Journal of Rural Development*, 16(4), 557–573.

Jayal, Niraja, Prakash and Sharma, eds., 2006. *Local Governance in India; Decentralisation and Beyond*. New Delhi: Oxford University Press.

Jha, S.N. and Mathur, P.C., eds., 1999. *Decentralisation and Local Politics: Readings in Indian Government and Politics* (2). New Delhi: Sage

John and Chathukulam, 1999. 'The Relationship Between Gram Panchayat and Gram Sabha', *Kukurshetra*, 48(1), 40–45.

John, Mary, J., 2007. 'Kerala's Gram Sabhas and People's Awareness'. *ISDA Journal*, 17 (3), 213–240.

Johnson, Craig, 2003. *Decentralisation in India: Poverty, Politics and Panchayati Raj*. Working Paper No. 199, Brighton: Overseas Development Institute.

——, 2001. 'Local Democracy, Democratic Decentralisation and Rural Development: Theories, Challenges and Options for Policy'. *Development Policy Review*, 19(4), 521–32.

Johnson, Craig, Deshingkar, Priya and Start, Daniel, 2005. 'Grounding the State: Devolution and Development in India's Panchayats'. *Journal of Development Studies*, 41 (6), 937–970.

Joseph and John, 2000. 'Gram Sabha Experience in Tamil Nadu; Difficult Road Ahead'. *Journal of Rural Development*, 20 (2), 253–272.

Joshi, G.V. and Shenoy, 1995. 'The Gram Sabha in Karnataka: Some Reflections and Reality'. *Quarterly Journal of All India Institute of Local Self Government*, 66 (3–4), 195–201.

Kohli, A., ed., 2009. *Democracy and Development in India*. New Delhi: Oxford University Press.

——, ed., 2001. *The Success of India's Democracy*. Cambridge: Cambridge University Press.

——, 1992, *Democracy and Discontent: India's Growing Crisis of Governability*, Cambridge: Cambridge University Press.

——, 1987. *The State and Poverty in India: The Politics of Reform*. Cambridge: Cambridge University Press.

Kothari, Rajni, 2005. *Rethinking Democracy*, Hyderabad: Orient Black Swan.

——, 1999. 'Issues in Decentralized Governance', in Jha and Mathur, eds.

——, 1998. *State Against Democracy. In Search of Humane Governance*. New Delhi: Ajanta.

Krishna, Anirudh, ed., 2008. *Poverty, Participation, and Democracy: A Global Perspective*. Cambridge: Cambridge University Press.

Kumar, Sanjoy and Corbridge, 2002. 'Programmed to Fail: Development Projects and the Politics of Participation'. *The Journal of Development Studies*, 39 (2), 73–103.

Kumar, Girish, 2006. *Local Democracy in India*. New Delhi: Sage.

Lieten, G K., 2003. *Power, Politics and Rural Development: Essay on India*. New Delhi: Manohar.

——, 1996. *Development, Devolution and Democracy*. New Delhi: Sage.

Lieten, G.K. and Srivastava, R., 1999. *Unequal Partners: Power Relations, Devolution and Development in Uttar Pradesh*. New Delhi: Sage.

Luckham, Robin, Goetz, Anne-Marie and Kaldor, Mary, 2000. *Democratic Institutions and Politics in Contexts of Inequality, Poverty, and Conflict: A Conceptual Framework*. Working Paper No 104, Brighton: Overseas Development Institute.

Maddick, Henry, 1970. *Panchayati Raj; A Study of Rural Local Government in India*. London: Orient Longman.

Maharatna, Arup, 2007. 'Population, Economy and Society in West Bengal since the 1970s'. *Journal of Development Studies*. 43 (8), 1381–1422.

Majumdar, Manabi, 2009. 'Democracy in Praxis: Two Non-Left Gram Panchayats in West Bengal'. *Economic & Political Weekly*, 28 February, 82–93.

Mallick, Ross, 1993. *Development Policy of a Communist Government*. Cambridge: Cambridge University Press.

Mandal, Amal, ed., 2005, *Rural Development in West Bengal*, New Delhi: Northern Book Centre.

Mandar, Harsh, 1999. 'Towards Direct Democracy: Legal Empowerment of Gram Sabha'. *Kurukshetra*, 48(1), 2–13.

Manor, James, 2004. 'Democratisation with Inclusion: Political Reforms and People's Empowerment at the Grassroots'. *Journal of Human Development*, 5 (1), 5–29.

——, 2003. 'Democratic Decentralisation in Two Indian States: Past and Present.' *The Indian Journal of Political Science*, 63 (1), 51–72.

——, 2001. 'Madhya Pradesh Experiment With Direct Democracy'. *Economic & Political Weekly*, March 3, 715–716.

——, 1999. *The Political Economy of Democratic Decentralisation*. Washington: The World Bank.

Meenakshisundaram, S.S., 1994. *Decentralisation in Developing Countries*. New Delhi: Concept.

Mohnan B., 2005. *Decentralizing the Leftist Way-Decentralised Governance and Participating Development: Issues, Constraints and Prospects*. New Delhi: Concept.

Mukarji, Nirmal and Bandyopadhyaya, 1993. *New Horizon for West Bengal's Panchayats: A Report for the Government of West Bengal*. Kolkata: Department of Panchayat.

Nambiar, Malini, 2001. 'Making the Gram Sabha Work'. *Economic & Political Weekly*, August 18, 3114–3117.

Namboodiri, Udayan, 2006. *Bengal's Night Without End*. New Delhi: India First Foundation.

Narayan, D., Chambers, R., Shah, M.K. and Petesch, P., 2000, *Voices of the Poor: Crying Out For Change*. Washington: The World Bank.

Oommen, John, 1999. 'Functioning of Gram Sabha in Kerala', in Choudhury and Jain, eds.

Palanithurai, G., 1999. 'Gram Sabha: a Civil Society at the Bottom'. in Choudhury and Jain, eds.

Palanithurai, G. and Ragupathy, 2006. *Functional Efficiency of Gram Sabha in Tamil Nadu*. New Delhi: Concept.

Planning Commission. *Vision 2020: Governance, Decentralisation and People's Participation*. New Delhi; Government of India.

Prasad, R.C., 1980. 'Local Government and Development in India'. *International Political Science Review*, 1(2), 265–299.

PRIA, 2001. *The State of Panchayat*. New Delhi: Samskriti. (Written by Rai, Nambiar, Paul, Singh and Sahni).

Rao, Vijayendra and Sanyal, Paromita, 2009. *Dignity Through Discourse: Poverty and the Culture of Deliberation in Indian Village Democracies*. Policy Research Working Paper No 4924, Washington: The World Bank.

Rau, S.K., 2001. 'Gram Sabha'. *Journal of Rural Development*, 20 (4), 779–803.

Reddy, G.R., 1989, 'The Politics of Accommodation: Caste, Class and Dominance in Andhra Pradesh', *in* Francine Frankel and Rao, M.S.A., eds. *Dominance and State Power in Modern India: Decline of a Social Order* (Vol. I), New Delhi: Oxford University Press.

Reddy, M.G., 2003. 'Status of Decentralised Local Bodies: Post-73rd Amendment Scenario'. *Economic & Political Weekly*, March 22, 1284–92.

Retna, Raj, ed., 2006. *Decentralised Governance and Poverty Reduction: Lesson From Kerala.* Thrissur: Kerala Institute of Local Administration.

Ribot, Jessie, C., 2004. *Waiting for Democracy: The Politics of Choice in Natural Resource Decentralisation*. Washington: World Resources Institute.

Rondinelli, D., McCullough, J.S. and R.W. Johnson, 1989. 'Analyzing Decentralisation Policies in Developing Countries: a Political Economy Framework', *Development and Change*, 20(1), 57–87.

Roy, A., Dey, N. and Singh, S., 2001. 'Demanding Accountability', *Seminar*, April,

Roy, S.N., 2001. Gram Sansad, Decentralised Planning and Participatory Development in West Bengal: The New CCA Strategy and Experiment', in Jain, S.P., ed.

Rudd, Arild Engelsen, 2003. *Poetics of Village Politics*. New Delhi: Oxford University Press.

Sen, Rajib and Yasin, 2007. 'People's Participation Through Decentralisation: A Study of the Gram Sansad Experiment in West Bengal'. *ISDA Journal*, 17 (3), 179–199.

Shah, Anwar, ed., 2006. *Local Governance in Developing Countries*. Washington: The World Bank,

Singh, A K., 1999. 'Gram Sabha Experience in Madhya Pradesh', in Choudhury and Jain, eds.

Singh, S., Sharma, P.K., 2007. *Decentralisation: Institution and Politics in Rural India*. New Delhi: Oxford University Press.

Sivaramkrishnan, K.C., ed., 2000. *Power to the People*. New Delhi: Konark.

Srivastava, K.B., 1999. *Strategies for Strengthening Panchayat in Karnataka*, Report of an Action Research Project. Hyderabad: National Institute of Rural Development.

Sundar, Ram, ed., 2007. *Panchayati Raj and Empowering People*. New Delhi: Kanishka.

Thorlind, Robert, 2001. *Development, Decentralisation and Democracy: Exploring Social Capital and Politicisation in Bengal Region*. Nordic Institute of Asian Studies.

UNDP, 2004. *Ideas and Contributions: Democracy in Latin America—Towards a Citizens' Democracy*. New York: United Nations Development Programme Report.

——, 2002. *Human Development Report: Deepening Democracy in a Fragmented World*. New York: United Nations Development Programme and Oxford University Press.

Venkatarangaiya, M. and Pattaviram, eds, 1969. *Local Government in India*. Bombay (Mumbai): Allied.

Webster, Neil, 1992. *Panchayati Raj and Decentralisation of Development Planning in West Bengal*. Calcutta (Kolkata): K.P. Bagchi.

——, 1990. 'Agrarian Relations in Burdwan District, West Bengal: From the Economics of Green Revolution to the Politics of Panchayati Raj'. *Journal of Contemporary Asia*, 20(2), 177–211.

William, Glyn, 1999. 'Panchayati Raj and Changing Micro Politics in West Bengal', in Rogaly, Harriss and Bose, eds. *Sonar Bangla: Agricultural Growth and Agrarian Change in West Bengal and Bangladesh*, New Delhi: Sage, 229–252.

William, Glyn, Veron, Corbridge and Srivastava, 2003. 'Participation and Power: Poor People's Engagement with India's Employment Assurance Scheme'. *Development and Change*, 34 (1), 163–192.

World Bank, 2007. *India: Rural Government and Service Delivery*. Washington.

Index